LANDO NORRIS

Ben Hunt has written for every major national newspaper in the UK over the past twenty years, covering football, snooker, golf, cricket and motor sport. He is now the Formula One correspondent and motor-sport columnist at the *Sun* newspaper.

BEN HUNT

LANDO NORRIS

A BIOGRAPHY

ICON

Published in the UK and USA in 2023 by
Icon Books Ltd, Omnibus Business Centre,
39–41 North Road, London N7 9DP
email: info@iconbooks.com
www.iconbooks.com

ISBN: 978-183773-012-4
eBook: 978-183773-013-1

Typesetting by SJmagic DESIGN SERVICES, India

Printed and bound in the UK

CONTENTS

Prologue .... **VII**

1   Early Promise **1**

2   The Formation of Team Norris **9**

3   Lando Morris? **15**

4   First Taste of F1 .... **25**

5   The Little Brother **45**

6   A New Deal **61**

7   Put on Hold **81**

8   A New Teammate **111**

9   Heartbreak in Russia **135**

10   The Monaco Move **151**

Lando Norris Professional Racing Record **173**

Acknowledgements **179**

PROLOGUE

It was a staggering lap that encompassed everything required from a modern F1 driver. Bravery. Vital radio communication. The mental capacity to make multiple changes to a car's braking and engine performance through various switch changes, all while travelling at 200 mph. Precision car placement. Racecraft. Plus, the ability to keep a cool head until crossing the finishing line. Only then, and perhaps it took a few moments longer than usual, was Lando Norris able to comprehend the outcome of his actions on what had been the final lap of the 2020 Austrian Grand Prix.

The release of the tension was something else. While the team's staff celebrated wildly in the garage, the car's radio transmission was filled with emotion.

'Yes boiiiiii!' shouted Norris, as the McLaren driver had delivered a near-perfect final lap to pip reigning world champion Lewis Hamilton to third place. It was Norris' first podium in Formula One, and it came in dramatic circumstances at the Red Bull Ring as the sport celebrated its post-pandemic return in the first race of 2020.

Just prior to starting the penultimate lap, Norris had been told by his race engineer Will Joseph that he was trailing Hamilton by 6.5 seconds; however, the Mercedes driver had a post-race time penalty of five seconds that would be added on to his total time. This meant that Norris had to make up 1.6 seconds on his fellow Brit if he was to achieve his goal of securing a top-three finish.

It started well as Norris squeezed past Sergio Pérez. Heading uphill and into Turn Three of the final lap of the spectacular 4.318-kilometre track set in the Styrian mountains, he was told by Joseph to change his engine setting, turning the power mode up to 'scenario seven'. Simultaneously, he had permission to use the overtake button, draining his car's battery pack to power the hybrid engine and deliver an extra 40 horsepower.

He made the apex at Turn Three and then changed the differential and brake bias, all the while trimming his McLaren in pursuit of Hamilton. The final two corners were right on the limit as Norris wrestled his car home, giving it his all. As he crossed the line, his team were already celebrating as engineer Joseph delivered the news.

'The gap was 4.8 [seconds], I think that's a podium,' he said hesitantly.

Norris has since claimed to be a little embarrassed by his wild celebration over the team's radio.

He was adamant he was not crying. Definitely not … Or maybe just a little …

'I remember everything from the last lap and a half. My engineer was telling me on the radio every few corners what I could do with my engine, what I could do with the car to unlock more potential and make it go quicker,' he said afterwards. 'It was a chance for the podium. I just knew I had to push as much as I could if I had the opportunity.'

Norris' whole career had been leading to this point. Through the ranks of karting and single-seaters to reach the pinnacle of motor sport. He was just twenty years old, becoming the third-youngest driver to ever stand on a grand prix podium – and the youngest British driver to do so.

He celebrated in suitable fashion, slamming his champagne bottle down onto the ground, sending a fizzy stream out of the top as he sprayed the contents into the air rather than down his throat. The moment was captured in a picture featuring Valtteri Bottas and Charles Leclerc, who are swigging from their bottles.

'There was one picture I saw of the three of us on the podium, the other two drivers are drinking away and I'm just pouring it over my head,' Norris told the BBC. 'I've put it to much better use in my eyes. I would say milk at the end of the day still tastes better!'

In his unconventional, refreshingly honest and brilliantly quick way, Lando Norris had announced himself as a future star of F1.

EARLY PROMISE

Lando Norris is one of the most exciting talents in Formula One, and he has rightly been identified as a future star. According to two-time F1 champion Emerson Fittipaldi, he 'has already established himself as what I call a potential world champion'. Nico Rosberg, who won the title in 2016, agrees that Britain's youngest-ever F1 driver 'has what it takes to be a world champion'.

These two former racers know their stuff, but the reality is there have always been more drivers dubbed future world champions in F1 than actual world champions. However, Lando Norris is rather special.

I have been fortunate to experience first-hand much of Lando's racing career, witnessing his rapid rise through the ranks to reach the pinnacle of motor sport. The highs and the lows, both on and off the track. How his interactions on social media have seen him attract a huge fan base as he has the unusual accolade of being one of the most universally popular F1 drivers of all time. Even in a dramatic finale to the 2021 season, he was caught up in the bitter rivalry between Max Verstappen and Lewis Hamilton, yet somehow, the young racer found himself in the position of being lauded by both competitors – and their staunch fans. His self-deprecating sense of humour has seen him stay true to his values and allowed him to find his voice in a sport that is often dominated by egos. He has spoken out on subjects, such as racism and mental health, that in the past have been taboo topics in the macho world of F1. During his time in F1, he has gone wheel-to-wheel with the champions to become the de facto team leader at McLaren, one of F1's most prestigious and historic teams.

Until now, the world title has eluded him, but surely it is only a matter of time.

Norris was born on 13 November 1999 in Bristol to parents Adam and Cisca. His mum, originally from the Flanders region of Belgium, is who Norris credits with coming up with his unique first name. He insists it has nothing to do with the character Lando Calrissian in the *Star Wars* movies, played by actor Billy Dee Williams. You may well remember Calrissian from the films, he was the original owner of the *Millennium Falcon* until he lost it in a bet to Han Solo.

Norris has an older brother, Oliver, who would also kart competitively between 2008 and 2014 with limited success. He now runs his own racing simulator business for professional drivers called Cool Performance that has sims stationed across the world. Norris also has two sisters named Cisca and Flo, the latter of whom is a showjumper and has enjoyed considerable success in her sport. His dad Adam is a wealthy businessman and serial entrepreneur. He was managing director of UK firm Pensions Direct at the age of 33 and effectively retired at 36 when he sold the business to become one of Bristol's wealthiest residents.

But it would be wrong to assume that Adam Norris came from wealth himself. Born in Yeovil in 1971, his father was a farmer and his mother was a teacher. He started working as a financial adviser in 1993 and then Pensions Direct, the pension arm of Hargreaves Lansdown in 1998. An article in *City A.M.* published in 2022 took Norris back to his days at Pensions Direct where he revealed he would secretly sleep at the firm to ensure he could get ahead. Utilising a shower at the office, he would work later than his colleagues and still be at his desk earlier than them the following morning.

'I had to try harder than everyone else,' he told Darren Parkin, 'I wasn't that good when I started, and I needed to work much more to get up to their level. I enjoyed my time there. I started in business very early and struggled to get anyone to believe my idea of selling pensions. Within three or four years, though, Hargreaves Lansdown became the UK's biggest pension company. People thought I was stupid at school, because I was at the bottom of the year. I also struggled with people's names. To this day I'm still no good at recalling people's names – I forget 99 per cent. I got tested for it at primary school, but knowing what was wrong didn't help – it just felt like dyslexia was another word for stupid. I hated school. Genuinely hated it. I didn't have a great time and, in a way, going to university wasn't any better. And going to work wasn't right either.'

Reading about Adam Norris' work ethic, it is clear to see how that has translated to his son's success. 'We still pinch ourselves,' he continues in the article after being asked about his son's racing career. 'I think he has an unimaginable life. But he works hard at it, and it's fascinating to watch how much he loves it. But it frightens the life out of me – the first few laps. There are shunts, but most of these things happen early in the race so you can relax a little. Well, maybe not relax, but you know what I mean. He's got a great team of people around him … and we've all said, "Who thought we'd ever be here?"'

Adam Norris is currently the CEO of Horatio Investments, based in Glastonbury – famous for its music festival, which is near the family home. He is also the founder of Pure Electric Ltd, a company that produces the electric scooters that have become increasingly popular on European streets in recent years, claiming he is 'good at spotting emerging trends' and wanted to help stop global warming by encouraging electric-powered mobility.

But it was conventional, petrol-powered motorbikes that got his two sons hooked on racing. When he was four, Lando started riding horses with his mum before his father bought him a quadbike. But he was then given a motorbike for his sixth birthday, which coincided with him starting to watch MotoGP. It was not until a visit to watch the Super 1 National Kart Championships at his local kart track around the same age that he became interested in four wheels rather than two. He was just seven when he first started racing competitively, and in 2008, at the age of eight, he joined the Super 1 Championships. The series has a record for producing some of the best British talent, with Lewis Hamilton, Jenson Button, David Coulthard, Alexander Albon, Dan Wheldon, Anthony Davidson and Jason Plato having competed in it. Lando claimed pole position at his first national event and was the youngest driver to ever get pole at a national meeting. Early in his first season, after overcoming some mechanical problems, he went on to join the Mick Barrett Racing team. At Mick Barrett, the team were using the Tony Kart chassis, which allowed Norris to be competitive against more experienced karters. Norris spent four years in the Cadet class making steady progress. In his first season he was ranked 35th, in his second he was up to fourteenth and in 2010 he was third in the championship and also won the 'O' Plate in that season, one of karting's most prestigious awards, at the Rotax Open Championship.

In 2011, Norris raced in the Kartmasters British Grand Prix, the Super 1 National Championship and the MSA British Championship. Around the same time, his father enlisted the help of Mark Berryman and Fraser Sheader to manage Lando and Oliver's fledgling careers in karting. Both men had experience in karting, with Sheader competing at 'a pretty high level' against the likes of Hamilton in his karting years. Despite being hailed as one of the most promising British talents, Sheader failed to reach the very top due to a lack of financial backing. After a stint managing the English team Maranello Kart and acting as driver coach for fellow racer Jack Harvey, he set up ADD management with Berryman in 2010, which is an agency that supports and nurtures young racing talent.

'Lando would have been eleven going into his twelfth year,' recalls Berryman when asked about his meetings with Norris. 'His dad approached us, and then at that point, we were looking after a couple of drivers who were making the transition from karts to cars and his dad felt like they needed some help. I'd already met Lando because I was doing some work for one of the race teams he was racing with at the time, Rotax. He was very quiet and for at least the first nine months he didn't listen to a word I said. His dad was pleased because he was winning loads, but I told him that Lando was not listening to a word I said. We were doing a great job for Olly because he started winning too, but Lando just wasn't listening. Eventually, he must have realised I was not going to leave him alone. For nine months, it was like breaking a horse and, after proving myself to him, he started to listen to me.'

It was clear early on that despite his obvious wealth Adam Norris would not be willing to pump in extortionate amounts of money to grow Lando's career. Berryman remembers a time when Adam told Lando that he needed to work harder and practise more, and although the young racer may not have liked it, it turned out that his dad was spot on. Sheader admits that the somewhat unconventional approach perfectly suited the principles of his newly formed company.

'One of the significant things from Adam's perspective was that he was not all about just buying the best kit all the time,' he says. 'Their ethos as a family was about developing Lando's talent from a young age and not trying to buy his way up through the categories, which really connected with what we were doing as a company. We were trying to develop drivers rather than just place them in teams, so it just meshed together perfectly. We sat down with Adam and he was all about developing and nurturing talent. It definitely gave us the opportunity to exercise what our philosophy was, and of course he was supported by the entire family, which must have had more than a bit to do with it! But from eleven years old, they weren't afraid of making things difficult to make Lando stronger and more adaptable.'

Norris' karting career quickly took off and, despite his initial reluctance to listen to Berryman, he was winning races. The family moved to Glastonbury, where he and Oliver attended the prestigious independent school Millfield – as day pupils rather than boarders. The school has an excellent reputation, even if Norris was not initially interested in being top of the class. It quickly became apparent that, like his father, he was not necessarily the most studious student. With the school's permission, Norris was granted leave to compete in karting. The sports-oriented Millfield school agreed and made provisions for a tutor to travel with both of the Norris brothers to ensure they would catch up on any lessons they missed. 'He started home-schooling from about fourteen,' says Berryman. 'The school and family were conscious that both brothers would be away from lessons and then required to catch up, so we had a tutor come with us to the races. Lando would be doing homework on the way to races or on the way back, although that soon stopped and we started doing it online.'

During the early years, Norris continued to get good results on the track, but he often did not agree with Berryman's advice and instead tried to do it his own way. 'He was really fast,' says Berryman, who remains in Norris' closely knit team and is usually with him during F1 race weekends. 'So even though he was not listening, he was still winning races. He was always really good in qualifying. We'd go to some of the kart races and I'd ask the team if they were cheating. I remember one race in the juniors and the same lap time would have put him sixth on the grid in the seniors and I assumed that it just could not be right. He was that quick. On other occasions, there would be times when it was wet and he would go wide round a corner. I'd tell him that he definitely needed to be closer to the curb, but he'd just go even wider. In the end, I just said to him, if you look at the lap times, if I am right you go quicker. If you are right, it stays the same, so you might just try it.

'But now he is the polar opposite. For instance, at the São Paulo Grand Prix in 2022, in the middle of the session, I texted Jon Malvern, his trainer, and Lando went out on track and tried something I had suggested to try straight away. Of all our drivers now, he is the best in terms of if you put something forward, he just does it. He might come back and say, "I tried it three times and it didn't work," or that it was good advice. But that is now one of his biggest strengths in terms of listening to input from others.'

Having the success and a management team behind him also drew the envy of his rivals, who were quick to highlight his father's wealth. But as both Sheader and Berryman point out, no driver on the F1 grid currently has got there without some form of financial backing. 'Some people in the sport are pretty good at trying to deceive people about how much wealth they have got,' says Sheader. 'Of course, there is a difference, some have more than others, that's obvious. But there are ones who still manage to continue for a very long time.'

'Anyone who is on the F1 grid, whether it is from personal wealth or from backing from a manufacturer, has got there through spending a similar amount of money to everyone else,' adds Berryman. 'So when we look at our total spend to go from A to B, it is actually cheaper than most people because they competed for years and we just managed to go bang, bang, bang [through the racing categories]. So we are on average in terms of spend. The reality is it costs money to get to F1. It doesn't matter where that money has come from, they have all paid to get there. Like with Hamilton, he had a lot of McLaren money behind him when he started.'

THE FORMATION OF TEAM NORRIS

Norris continued to win more races and rattled through the different categories. In 2012, he raced in seven competitions, finishing second in the Super 1 National Championship in the Rotax Mini Max class and winning the Formula Kart Stars also in the Mini Max class. During the same season, he started competing in the WSK Final Cup driving for Ricky Flynn Motorsport in the junior division, now that he was old enough. The other notable moment from the year was a tweet he made in May 2012. A twelve-year-old Norris wrote: 'The first day of school boring but its [sic] May Fair so probably better plus my mum is doing pancakes so yum yum.' The wonderfully innocent post later resurfaced in 2020 when the Formula 1 Twitter account resurrected it, prompting a reaction from Norris on the social media channel. He wrote: 'Finally, I can make an announcement!! I wanted to tell you all for the last hour, I had a pancake for breakfast with a strawberry on top.' This was effectively the starting point for what was to become Lando's way of expressing himself online and subsequently growing his fan base.

Things really started to take off in Norris' karting career in 2013. Racing for Ricky Flynn, who are based in Waltham Abbey in the UK, he had a stellar year winning both the CIK FIA

European Championship and the International Super Cup as well as the WSK Euro Series. He was second in the WSK Super Master Series, but such was the acceleration of his development, he also competed in the CIK-FIA World Championship in the junior series, finishing in fourth place. At the same time, future F1 world champion Max Verstappen was competing in the World Championship in the KF2 class – basically a feeder league for drivers aged fourteen and up that was a division above Norris – where he was third overall.

The following year Norris progressed to the KF2 class and did so with yet more considerable success. He was third in the CIK-FIA European Championship, and more importantly, he won the CIK-FIA World Championship, making history as the youngest world champion at just fourteen years old. As if that was not enough, with his education effectively over, he was also able to race in the Ginetta Junior Championship. The Ginetta series is an altogether different discipline to karting. Racing in Ginetta G40s sports cars in support of the British Touring Car Championship calendar, Lando took in some of the UK's premier racing circuits, such as Brands Hatch, Donington and Silverstone. He finished the season in a credible third place after taking time to adjust to car racing.

Championship-winner Jack Mitchell and Norris' teammate James Kellet, who was second, had both raced and won in the championship the previous season. Mitchell had started the campaign on the front foot and won the first four races, but once Norris was up to speed by the ninth round, he proved to be the driver to beat. He took five consecutive pole positions and a further three in the remaining seven races. In total, he took four wins and eleven podiums to clinch the Rookie Cup, which underlined his growing reputation as a future star. Sheader says he was guiding Norris into different types of racing to make him a better all-round driver. 'It's probably one of the most significant factors,' he says, 'because Adam was so open minded to making Lando adaptable and able to drive a broad spectrum of cars, we were able to do that. Most drivers can't do that – jumping between different cars – but Lando has practised it from such a young age. He was going between slippery UK circuits on hard tyres straight to European circuits on grippy tyres. Him doing eight big international kart races was not easy, but he'd been training and we had also been able to prepare him. Some of the teams did not like it because they felt he would be winning even more if he concentrated on one championship, but we were looking at the bigger picture and producing an F1 driver.'

Norris had two crucial meetings in 2014. The first was with Jon Malvern, the fitness and conditioning coach who would remain by his side as he climbed the ranks and into F1. The second was with Trevor Carlin, boss of the Carlin Motorsport team, who had been watching Norris' sensational rise. Speaking to Carlin in 2020 after Norris' first F1 podium, he recalled how the fifteen-year-old was only focused on racing – and nothing has changed since. 'He was great fun and at certain times he would like his own space and sit in a corner, pull his hoodie up and play with his phone,' he said. 'The fact is, he was constantly driving a real car or a simulator. His poor old mum! Lando would do a test day with us and go home about 8 o'clock at night after a long day. His mum would ask him how his day had been but Lando would just grab his dinner and go and sit on his simulator and go racing again online!'

Carlin offered Norris a place in his team for the 2015 season, competing in the newly established MSA Formula Championship, which is now known as the F4 British Championship. The series took in the tracks that Norris had competed in during the Ginetta Junior Championship, so he would benefit from the experience he gained the previous year. He took eight wins, ten pole positions and fifteen podiums to win the championship, clinching the title at Brands Hatch. He was also signed up for the ADAC Formula 4 Championship for three of the eight rounds that made up the championship. He competed in three races in each of the legs at Spa, Nürburgring and Hockenheim, winning once in Spa, with second places in the other two circuits. On top of that, he also drove in the Italian Formula 4 Championship for the legs in Monza, Mugello and Imola as he gained more racing on tracks that feature on the F1 calendar.

Norris' core team of Berryman, Sheader and Malvern soon expanded with the arrival of a figure who would have a huge impact on his racing career. By the end of 2016, Lando had proved his credentials beyond doubt. He won the Eurocup Formula Renault 2.0 by a whopping 53 points thanks to five wins and twelve podiums in fifteen races. He won the Formula Renault 2.0 Northern European Cup by 41 points with a victory at Silverstone and two wins in Spa, the highlights of his six victories, and a combined total of eleven podiums. He added those titles to the Toyota Racing Series championship he'd won earlier in the year in New Zealand. In doing so, he became the first European to win it and did so with a race to spare, amassing six wins, eight poles and five fastest laps. Somehow he also managed to fit in the time to race in the BRDC British F3 Championship where he competed in four legs of the season, taking four wins and eight podiums in the eleven races he entered. Finally, there were also three races in the FIA Formula 3 European Championship at the final event of the year in Hockenheim as he got in some early practice for the following season.

Midway through the year, Sheader had a chance meeting with Zak Brown, co-owner of United Autosports, a sports-car racing team founded by Brown and Richard Dean, to discuss having another driver brought onto the books at ADD

Management. The two met at Circuit Paul Ricard in France in August where Norris was racing in the Eurocup and Brown's team were competing in the four-hour Le Castellet race in the European Le Mans Series. 'We had built ourselves up and we were very confident in terms of the driver development, and they were flourishing in their junior careers,' Sheader says. 'But we knew we needed some commercial depth within the company, so we brought Zak in to our side for a short period to help bridge the gap. It was more about perception. He did not have to do too much to make a big difference, but that is his role because he is at that sort of level … I explained how he was the guy who could help us, plus we said that we thought Lando was pretty handy, so it was an ideal scenario for all of us. He was able to support us when it came to the doors that we had already opened and give us some stamp of authority in the paddock.' Brown agreed to a commercial deal between the two parties, and fortunately for ADD Management and Norris, later that year he was also announced as executive director of McLaren Technology Group.

In April 2018, Brown moved even higher into the ranks of F1 as he was promoted to chief executive officer of McLaren Racing as part of an operational restructure.

ADD Management would also enlist the help of Martyn Pass, the experienced journalist and publicist who had been working with Lance Stroll in the European F3 series. 'Contact was made for me to do Lando's PR in the same championship,' Pass explains, 'I was at some of Lando's European races, so I got to see some of his early races. I was struck by his incredible determination to achieve success. Finishing first was the only thing that mattered. If he was second, he would be massively disappointed. Over the next two years, I was with Mark and Jon and we would stay at the same hotel and they formed a very solid team. I did about ten weekends with Lando in 2016, which consisted of 30 races, and I wrote the previews, reports and arranged interviews with the media. Only once in the three years did he not give me a direct quote, and that was at Pau in France. He was a country mile ahead in the race. He was pushing on, as he would do because he wanted to win by the biggest margin, when he broke his suspension on a kerb and crashed out. It cost him victory and he was crestfallen. I walked into the paddock, and he was in the Carlin transporter and was upset and annoyed with himself, so much so that he did not want to give me a quote.'

Pass would go on to follow Norris into F2 and oversaw his F1 debut. 'Lando was devoted to achieving his goal 24/7,' he says, 'winning and reaching F1 was all that mattered to him and his life revolved around a pattern set out for him by Mark. He is a lovely guy but totally focused. He is a GP winner of the future and ultimately a world champion, but as we all know, you have to have the right car at the right time.' Meanwhile, Norris' achievements had not gone unnoticed, and at the end of 2016 he was presented with the *Autosport* British Club Driver of the Year Award in recognition of his success as his professional career started to gather momentum.

LANDO MORRIS?

'Lando Morris? He is a young driver, right?' Charlotte Sefton asked the receptionist at McLaren's factory in February 2017. Sefton was senior communications manager for McLaren's F1 team – and she would later play an instrumental part in Norris' career. She had gone to speak to the receptionist of the McLaren Technology Centre in Woking, or MTC as it is more widely known.

The MTC is a semi-circular structure that has large glass walls and sits opposite a manmade lake that was designed by architect Norman Foster. It was opened in May 2003 at a cost of around £300 million and is home to McLaren's 800 staff. It was the dream of Ron Dennis, the former owner, CEO, chairman and founder of McLaren Group, who was relieved of his management role in 2016, a development that opened the door for Zak Brown's arrival.

Dennis, who had a long and successful career at McLaren, had an eye for detail to the extreme. There are amazing stories about how every screwhead in the building has been left with the slot in a vertical position so that it does not gather dust. 'The temperature in the canteen is also allegedly set at a specific figure that is optimal for digestion. Given their intricate design and alignment, should any of the floor tiles in the building be damaged, the whole lot would need replacing. Heaven forbid that one of the many cars on display on the Boulevard – the impressive museum-esque display of McLaren race cars on the ground floor of the building – would have an oil leak.

'I was doing a filming event on the Boulevard,' says Sefton. 'I went downstairs to go speak to the person who sits by the doors at reception. I explained that I had some filming going on in the afternoon and that I needed to make sure there was no one on the Boulevard at that time. I wanted to make sure that everyone coming and going out of the building knew it was not accessible. I was told that all the tours had been moved or cancelled so everything was fine apart from one guest arriving. He was called "Lando Morris", but I did not need to worry about him because he would come straight in and go up the lift to see Zak. I was not familiar with his name, so I doubled-checked the spelling. The person on reception added that he was a VIP guest and that it was all being kept top secret, so I was not to say anything.'

Sefton's curiosity got the better of her, and she searched for 'Lando Morris' on the internet. She realised that it was Lando Norris who was coming to visit Brown. 'I found Lando Norris and wondered, "Is it this guy?" I thought, "Oh, he's seventeen, looks a bit geeky." I guessed that McLaren were finally setting up a draft programme for young drivers, so I thought that it sounded exciting. Later, I was on the Boulevard and this shy kid got out of a Mini and walked in. He said "hello" and for some reason I was expecting him to be French. I asked him to be quiet as we were filming, and he went up in the lift to Zak's office. I was like, "Is this the future? Who knows?"'

Little did Sefton know that a few days later, Norris would be confirmed as a junior driver for McLaren. Brown's links to ADD Management were not widely known at this point, and the announcement was not deemed to be big news. For journalists, all the focus was on the car launches for the 2017 season, so the signing of a seventeen-year-old as a junior driver went by largely unnoticed. At the time, Brown hailed Norris as a 'fabulous prospect'. He said Norris had 'blown the doors off his rivals in not one but three highly competitive race series' in 2016 and 'capped that by establishing himself as the clear winner of the McLaren Autosport BRDC Award'. He added: 'It was an impressively mature performance, and we'll be developing him this year as part of our simulator team, whereby he'll be contributing directly and importantly to our Formula 1 campaign at the same time as honing and improving his technical feedback capabilities.'

Norris kicked off the European 2017 Formula 3 season in style, winning the opening race at Silverstone for Carlin. Not only did he win the race, he also took pole position and set the fastest lap in a clean sweep. Victories in Monza, Norisring, Spa, Zandvoort and the Nürburgring took his tally to nine wins, eight poles, and he finished on the podium in twenty of the 30 races that season. With such sensational form, he took the title at the first attempt – and with two races to spare. It was his fifth racing championship title in four years.

It was all hugely impressive. Norris had arrived on the scene and dominated. And McLaren were impressed too. They offered him a chance to test their current F1 car in the mid-season test at the Hungaroring immediately after the 2017 Hungarian GP. While most of the paddock heads off for a summer break, the mid-season test provides an opportunity for teams to get some crucial running time, with testing being extremely limited during the rest of the season.

But it was not only a chance to test out new parts on the car, it also offered teams the opportunity to blood youngsters, judge their lap times and also assess the feedback they provided to their engineers. It is all very well being quick, but the ability to suggest improvements to the car is another skill that is absolutely essential for young up-and-coming drivers.

'That summer,' recalls Sefton, 'I was like, "Oh, there's that kid again." He was in Hungary too and by that point, we had seen him around the building and knew he was part of the Young Driver Programme. I did not expect it to be happening so soon, but suddenly he was offered the opportunity to drive an F1 car, so by then we were like, "Oh wow, this kid is the new hotshot." Ahead of the young driver test in Hungary, we did some media work with him and he was like an absolute rabbit in headlights. There is a picture somewhere and it is of Lando and a massive crowd of journalists, and he just looks like a rabbit in headlights.'

But his performance in Hungary was excellent. Taking over from Stoffel Vandoorne, who had driven the previous day, Norris split the two Ferrari drivers and finished just 0.2 seconds behind Sebastian Vettel, who was leading the F1 championship.

McLaren's racing director Eric Boullier praised Norris and hailed the teenage sensation as he quickly got up to speed with the team's F1 car.

'Lando impressed us all with his maturity, professionalism and speed and has got to grips very quickly with the car in only his first outing in the MCL32,' gushed Boullier. 'His feedback with the engineers has been valuable and accurate, and he's certainly an asset to our test-driver line-up – not to mention a potential star of the future.'

After wrapping up the European Formula 3 season on 15 October, three weeks later, Norris was confirmed as the official McLaren test and reserve driver for the 2018 season.

'Lando has been a member of the McLaren Young Driver Programme since the start of 2017, and today's announcement crowns a hugely impressive twelve months for the seventeen-year-old,' said the press release. There was no doubt that his time in the simulator, coupled with his impressive F1 test debut at the Hungaroring had convinced McLaren to promote him as understudy to Fernando Alonso and Vandoorne. In the press release, Brown, who was McLaren's technology group executive director at the time, described Lando as an 'outstanding young talent … undoubtedly carving himself a reputation as one of the very best up-and-coming single-seater drivers in the world'. His final line in the release simply said: 'We are all extremely keen to help him achieve his goal of racing in Formula 1.' However, Boullier was a little more reserved, concluding that Norris would get 'plenty of opportunity to observe, learn and participate throughout 2018' so that he is 'fully prepared, if needed, to step into Fernando or Stoffel's shoes'.

Still, Lando's season was not over. In preparation for his new role, McLaren had lined him up for a special Pirelli tyre test in São Paulo following the 2017 Brazil Grand Prix. After making the twelve-hour flight, plus the couple of hours it takes to go from the São Paulo Guarulhos airport to the Hilton São Paulo Morumbi Hotel, he was relaxing in the bath when he got the news that his trip had been a waste of time. The tyre test had been cancelled for security reasons after eight members of the Mercedes team were robbed at gunpoint after leaving the circuit on Friday night. Pirelli staff were also targeted following the race on the Sunday. While nobody was hurt, the security concerns were significant, especially with a reduced police presence compared to the GP weekend. It proved to be a long way to go to have a bath – not to mention it was also Lando's eighteenth birthday weekend.

He subsequently flew to Macau, via Paris and Shanghai, to take part in the Macau Grand Prix where he finished second place following an accident between the leaders on the final lap. Even then his 2017 schedule was not over, for he still had one more race to complete, and one that would see him move further into the limelight, as he made his Formula 2 debut at the Abu Dhabi GP, replacing Ralph Boschung for the race at the Yas Marina Circuit.

It is rare that F1 teams make their reserve and test driver available to the F1 media. It is even more rare to say they'd have a reason to do so, so when Norris was introduced to the Fleet Street contingent for the first time, there was genuine intrigue among the press pack.

It was November 2017 at the Abu Dhabi Grand Prix. Alonso and Vandoorne were driving for the team at the time, and they had had a poor season, as the team continued to suffer reliability issues with their Honda power unit.

Off track, McLaren were obviously looking towards the future as they invited the press to officially meet Norris. The majority of those who attended were aware of his record in the lower categories but many had not seen him actually race.

Norris had been briefed by McLaren, as is usual, especially in these circumstances. Sefton and her excellent and experienced colleague Silvia Frangipane, who would later leave the team to work as head of communications at Scuderia Ferrari, provided the warnings.

'I've got a picture of him,' says Sefton, 'and he's just sat there, and he's got his team kit on. We had to sit him down beforehand and read him all the warnings and told him to talk about his own ambitions but that we would not be putting words in his mouth.'

For the press introduction, we were sat down in the McLaren hospitality unit, inside and away from the heat and the hectic throng of people working or trotting around the paddock outside in search of selfies. Around eight or nine of us were sat around a table, and it quickly became apparent that Lando was understandably nervous.

As is often the case with young British drivers, the comparison was made with Hamilton, and he was asked questions about the former McLaren driver. There was one particularly awkward exchange when one reporter asked if he was in contact with Lewis and whether he had received any congratulatory message from him after his appointment at McLaren. Norris was baffled, why would Lewis Hamilton, who was now at Mercedes, be sending him congratulations about a reserve driver role at McLaren?

But the questions kept on coming as the obvious parallels between the two were highlighted – both had achieved success; both were young when they were signed by the famous UK manufacturer; both were also incredibly highly regarded talent-wise.

One journalist asked Lando if he had a picture of Lewis on his bedroom wall when he was growing up, and his reply was wonderfully honest. He would have made all of the headlines if he had answered in the affirmative, but he replied truthfully, stating that it was in fact a picture of Valentino Rossi, the Italian MotoGP rider, who adorned his walls when he was a kid.

'I never had a picture of Lewis on my wall growing up,' he said, 'but he is a driver I look up to and you can aspire to be like him and admire his speed and talent – because he is one of the best. You want to win as many races as him and be on pole as much as he has. So he is someone I looked up to – but never wanted to be like.' Further questions followed, including one asking if he had received any tips from any current or former drivers on the grid. Again, his response was refreshingly honest. 'I don't think I need to speak to any of the British drivers for advice,' he said, 'but if I did, it would be Jenson [Button]. He has been around McLaren for a while, and I think he would be a good person to talk to.' It was a solid answer, and he then went on to reveal that it was his goal to get an F1 seat in 2019, despite the current McLaren line-up of Alonso and Vandoorne.

In the twenty-minute interview, there were two other answers that were particularly memorable. The first was a reply to a question about whether he would be leaving the family home in Somerset to move closer to the McLaren's Woking HQ. He revealed that he would be moving in with another rookie racer called Sacha Fenestraz, a French–Argentine driver who was the same age. This meant cutting ties to his family and learning to live on his own. Norris added: 'I'll still go home – mum wants me to come home all the time – but I can't iron, so I'll have to give it to Sacha!' And then, there was a question about where his Christian name had come from. He grinned and said: 'It's not from *Star Wars*. Mum just made it up. But I suppose it's good being a bit different.'

In that short encounter, it had become clear that Norris was going to be himself whenever he faced the media. One of my press colleagues left the interview and declared that Lando was 'nice, but with not too much about him', however, for me, it had become clear that if he was going to make it to F1, Lando would be doing things with the media his way.

But before he could even think about progressing to F1, Norris was committed to the F2 championship. For 2018, he would return to race with Carlin, but at the end of 2017, he still had two races to complete with Campos Racing. This was simply used as a way for him to get some extra experience in racing in F2 and it was a wise move by his management team, who had done the same in 2016 and signed him up for the final F3 race of the year at Hockenheim. The event in Abu Dhabi saw him retire in the feature race and finish thirteenth in the sprint race in what was an unspectacular end to an otherwise impressive year.

FIRST TASTE OF F1

The 2018 F2 championship was split over twelve rounds with two races each weekend – one sprint and one feature race. Moving back to the Farnham-based Carlin made a lot of sense for Norris. He would gain further experience on the tracks that form part of the F1 schedule, and the location of the team's HQ made it ideal for him to commute from nearby Addlestone.

Having just won the F3 title, he would now be up against a much tougher field. Another young British rising star, George Russell, was driving for ART along with fellow Brit Jack Aitken. The Thai–British racer Alexander Albon and Canadian Nicholas Latifi were paired at DAMS and the Dutchman Nyck de Vries was picked by Prema. Brazilian racer Sérgio Sette Câmara was in the other Carlin car, and he already had one season of F2 under his belt. He had also previously been on the Red Bull Racing Driver Programme. Norris had his work cut out and he knew it.

He had come close to winning the Macau Grand Prix in November 2017, finishing second behind Dan Ticktum. Afterwards, he complained that he only had himself to blame. 'I came to Macau to win, and in some ways I didn't prepare for it as much as I should have done,' he said. 'Maybe I could have done – because I was focusing on other things.'

Speaking ahead of the new season, Norris was under no illusions about the scale of the task ahead of him. He was measured and cautious about his expectations. 'I'm going into 2018 unquestionably aiming to achieve more success by winning races,' he said. 'But 2018 will also be a big learning year. Getting experience of the increased power, enhanced aerodynamics, the [Pirelli] tyres, the mandatory pit stops and competing at new tracks like Bahrain, Baku and Sochi.

'It's an educational year, I'll be new to Formula 2 while Carlin is returning after a season out of the category. I'll also be up against some very experienced F2 drivers. I'm hopeful it will work to our advantage that 2018 sees a newly designed car being raced for the first time since 2011. It'll be my fourth year competing with Carlin. Trevor heads up a great operation and I feel part of the family there. It's a friendly environment and one in which I feel very comfortable.'

He certainly looked comfortable as he took victory in the season-opener in Bahrain. Both Norris and Russell, two championship rookies, took the front row on the grid, with Norris starting P1 and Russell P2, and with Albon and de Vries qualifying just behind them.

For Albon, Norris set himself apart from the rest of the grid during qualifying.

'He pulled away immediately,' reflected Albon when asked about his first experience of competing with Norris in F2. 'I already knew he had some speed but he had slightly different preparation to most people. He was very structured, he had a team around him and they ensured he was ready for the next category he raced in. That was very impressive. It almost created the benchmark for people to follow. You see it now in junior drivers. They have this way of getting ready for the next year and hitting it hard. He came in as a rookie but was a very, very complete driver for someone who was so young in age but also experienced.

'I knew he was quick, so while I was not surprised, I was amazed to see how quickly he got on top of it, even more so when he got to Formula One, because you cannot really prepare for that, and yet he went and nailed it. It was impressive.

The 2018 F2 season saw a new design for the cars, which looked great under the spotlights in Bahrain on a 5.412-kilometre track set in the desert. A new chassis and engine package prompted the biggest shake-up in the series' history. The old chassis, which had been used since 2011, was replaced by the Dallara F2 2018 and powered by a 3.4-litre V6 single turbocharged engine developed by Mecachrome. The changes threatened to even the playing field, and from the very first practice session, it was obvious that this was indeed the case.

In qualifying, Russell set the early pace in his ART and then found even more time on his second run and was sitting at the top of the time sheets by over half a second. But it was Norris who took pole and the four bonus points with just three minutes of the session to go, despite making a slight error by running wide at the last turn.

However, there were no mistakes in the feature race as Norris converted his pole position with a dominant display. He crossed the line with an eight-second lead over his teammate Câmara to get the season off to a flying start. From P2, Russell finished down in fifth place. As for the sprint race, Norris was able to make his way up from eighth on the grid to fourth place, while Artem Markelov took the chequered flag and Câmara was third. Russell endured a miserable Sunday, finishing down in nineteenth.

At the next race in Azerbaijan, Norris was again quick in qualifying and posted the second-quickest time behind Albon in what was enough to secure P2 on the grid for the feature race. But this time, there was no repeat of the flying start he got in Bahrain as he stalled on the grid, which resulted in a start from the pit lane. He managed to come back to finish in sixth place, while Albon converted his pole into victory.

In the sprint race, Norris dropped one place from his grid position and took fourth, while Russell scored his first win of the season. The result meant that Norris led the championship with 55 points and Albon was second on 41. However, Norris was left reflecting on what had been a disappointing weekend. Writing in his blog on Sky Sports, he said: 'Sitting here at the airport waiting for my flight back to London, it's 24 hours since yesterday's second race in Baku but I still can't hide my disappointment.

'I could have done better in both Azerbaijan races. OK, I started Saturday's Feature Race with a nine-point lead after a win and a fourth place in the first two races in Bahrain and I'll get to Barcelona with an increased fourteen-point advantage. It's more points but not the amount I'd wanted. The Carlin Dallara could have been better and I made too many mistakes which cost me possible podiums in both races.'

Norris took two podiums in Barcelona in the next leg, despite starting the feature race in eighth. He was again able to make up places on Sunday, going from sixth to third, and he left Barcelona on 80 points, thirteen points ahead of Albon, while Russell had moved into third in the championship on 62 points in what was shaping up to be an exciting battle between the trio.

In Monaco, Norris finished sixth in the feature race, despite starting in seventeenth on the grid as he defied expectations following a three-place grid drop for being found to have impeded Albon during qualifying. In the sprint, Norris took his first Monaco podium and ten championship points, finishing third, while both Russell and Albon failed to finish the race.

By this time, Lando's performances were getting noticed, and on 6 June 2018, I ran a story in the *Sun* explaining how he was attracting the attention of Toro Rosso, who were considering the Brit as a replacement for the New Zealand driver Brendon Hartley, who was not making much impact at the Red Bull second team. Norris was at the centre of a tug of war, with Toro Rosso keen to fast-track him to F1, as they had done with world champions Vettel and Verstappen. However, the move was subsequently blocked by McLaren and Toro Rosso were urged to go elsewhere.

Two disappointing races in Paul Ricard followed, but Lando was back on the podium at the Red Bull Ring in Austria. His blog on Sky Sports once again provided an insight into how he was beginning to cope with the race schedule, which included triple-headers – three races on consecutive weekends.

'Paul Ricard, Red Bull Ring and Silverstone on consecutive weekends makes it an incredibly busy time for me and the entire Carlin team,' he said. 'I was knackered last Monday having got delayed flying back from Marseille but still needed to get my racing gear washed. I was on the simulator on Tuesday preparing for Austria, Jon came around to my place to work on my neck, before flying out to Austria on Wednesday morning.'

Triple-headers had found their way onto the F1 schedule as the calendar grew – by running three races together it allowed the sport to fulfil agreements with the circuits and broadcasters in an already congested schedule. By keeping three races together, and largely close geographically – France, Austria and the UK – there was an argument that it made more sense logistically and financially given that the teams simply moved the cars and equipment from track to track via road rather than via their respective factories.

Norris was looking forward to racing at the Red Bull Ring, it being a track he had performed well at in the past, having tasted victory there in Formula Renault and coming second in Formula 3. He arrived in Austria and took part in a feature with a reporter from *F1 Racing* magazine, who hitched a lift with him to the track in a McLaren 570S road car. His reputation was beginning to grow and a number of interviews with mainstream media had been lined up for him, which is pretty rare for an F2 driver. However, on the track, he struggled to match Russell, who was setting the early pace. A change in set-up improved things for qualifying and he was able to finish in P2, but crucially, his old foe Russell was still marginally ahead of him.

A slight change to the start added another element into the mix as F2 organisers decided to replace the usual standing starts with rolling starts behind the safety car for the opening two rounds. Many drivers had struggled with stalling problems on the starting grid in previous races, plus there was a big crash in an F3 race at the Norisring, so the change made sense. It worked for Norris as he was able to make a good start before pitting on lap six for fresh tyres. A couple of safety car periods hampered his progress, and he was forced to spend time conserving his tyres before a late push in the closing laps saw him secure second place behind Russell.

However, Sunday's sprint race did not go to plan. After overheating his tyres, he lost grip and became a sitting duck, slumping to an eleventh-place finish. Dejected, he flew home to the UK knowing his failure to look after those Pirelli tyres had cost him valuable points, as Russell's second-place finish was enough to see him replace Norris as the championship leader for the first time in the season.

The final race in the triple-header was at Silverstone, the home of the British Grand Prix. For the first time in a number of years – probably since Hamilton's days in GP2 – the home fans were witnessing something special in terms of home-grown talent coming through the ranks in the form of Norris, Russell and Albon, who were all vying for the F2 title. But while Russell and Albon were able to shine at Silverstone, Norris was left reflecting on another missed opportunity. Russell took pole ahead of Albon, but their fortunes were reversed in the feature race with Albon taking the chequered flag. Norris finished a lowly tenth. In the sprint race, he scored a podium at his home race, but the joy was tempered with Russell finishing second, while German racer Max Günther took top spot on the podium. However, the race will mostly be remembered for a collision between Trident teammates Arjun Maini and Santino Ferrucci. Ferrucci was accused of deliberately ramming the back of Maini's car on the cool-down lap, and he was slapped with a two-race ban by the FIA. Ten days later, he was axed by Trident.

Norris clawed back some crucial points in Hungary as he finished second and fourth, while Russell was hampered with a clutch problem that saw him fail to finish the feature race and he could only manage eighth in the sprint. Both Brits were then named as drivers for the test that followed the GP weekend at the Hungaroring. Norris would test for McLaren and Russell for Mercedes. Although there is not much to be read into in-season testing, it was interesting to see that the two drivers were closely matched in the time sheets on day one, with Norris fourth-quickest overall and Russell fifth. On day two, given Mercedes' car advantage over McLaren, it was no surprise to see that this order was reversed, but it was a surprise to see Russell go quickest of the lot. Norris was seventh for the day, although he was on the slower soft tyre, while those ahead of him were using the ultra-soft and hyper-soft tyres.

Norris' F2 championship hopes may have been slipping away, but McLaren had seen enough to be suitably impressed, so in the middle of the season, and somewhat fittingly given his mum's links to Belgium, he was handed his first run in an F1 session at the Belgian GP at Spa.

It is not unusual for teams to hand opportunities to their reserve drivers, but it was clear that given his results in Formula 2, McLaren were keen to see how he would cope during a proper F1 event and whether he was cut out for a race seat the following season.

He had impressed when he tested the MCL33 following the Hungarian Grand Prix in 2017, and he was therefore getting another opportunity behind the wheel, starting with a 90-minute session in Spa 2018. The team's sporting director at the time Gil de Ferran also hinted that Norris could get further opportunities later in the season, with eight F1 races to come after Belgium.

'This weekend will be the first time that our reserve driver Lando will drive the MCL33 during a race weekend, as he steps into Fernando's car for FP1 on Friday,' de Ferran said. 'This is not only part of his ongoing development, but also the evaluation and performance evolution of the car. We'll be taking a strategic view race by race at where else this might be beneficial for us over the coming grands prix.'

De Ferran's words came at a time when McLaren knew that Fernando Alonso would be leaving the team – and F1 – at the end of the season to be replaced by Carlos Sainz, who was leaving Renault.

However, there was an obvious question mark over Stoffel Vandoorne's future. The Belgian racer had been with McLaren since February 2013 when he was signed as part of the Young Driver Programme, and almost eleven months later, he was confirmed as the team's third driver while he juggled his time racing in GP2 with ART Grand Prix.

Vandoorne had an exceptional junior career, and it was obvious why he caught McLaren's eye. His results in his first season in GP2 – four wins, four poles and ten podiums – saw him finish as runner-up in his debut season in the series. He returned to GP2 in 2015 and won the championship thanks to seven wins and sixteen podiums across 21 races. Despite his success in GP2, he could not progress from the series as McLaren did not have a vacancy in F1 – with Button and Alonso racing for the team.

However, Vandoorne was given a chance in 2016 – for one race, the Bahrain Grand Prix – when Alonso was ruled out after a medical examination. At the season-opening Australian Grand Prix in Melbourne, Alonso clipped the rear of Esteban Gutierrez's car as they approached Turn Three at speed. Alonso thudded into the left-hand wall, but the momentum sent his car into a barrel roll across the gravel before it came to rest against the far tyre wall. Amazingly, he clambered out from the wreckage. However, he sustained injuries that were not initially obvious, and he consequently failed the medical on the eve of the Bahrain GP, with broken ribs and a pneumothorax, and had to be replaced by Vandoorne for the race. The Belgian managed to finish in a credible tenth place.

The following season in 2017, Vandoorne did get his race seat as a replacement for the retiring Jenson Button – the same season Norris would win the Formula 3 European Championship. However, with McLaren and Honda struggling for performance and reliability, the Belgian was only able to muster a handful of points, and for all his talent, he was never really offered a competitive car to show off his true ability. By the end of 2017, questions about his future in the team had begun to circulate.

Understandably, Norris' situation at McLaren had attracted media attention, and it was no surprise to see Sky Sports F1 running his 'F2 Diary' blog on their website, which offers some insight into his first weekend in F1 at the 2018 Belgian GP.

Unsurprisingly, in the post, Norris tactfully avoided mentioning how he was actually the quicker of the two drivers in a head-to-head with Vandoorne.

'I arrived at Spa on Wednesday,' Norris wrote, 'having driven over to Belgium with my trainer Jon. He drove and I watched Netflix! I'd had a nice break, which was good as I knew the next few days were going to be pretty tough with me doing FP1 in the McLaren on Friday in addition [to] the normal F2 stuff.'

'Spa is my favourite track so I was really looking forward to racing there again. Eau Rouge into Raidillon plus Pouhon, a tricky double apex left, are the stand-outs for me like most drivers. I'd gone pretty well in the past there in F4, Renault and F3. Weather conditions can be changeable and after the first part of the feature race in Hungary, I was quite happy if we would have rain again. Thursday was pretty full-on with pre-event briefings at McLaren, with Carlin engineers and the F2 driver's briefing going through until around 7.30pm.

'I was at the track by around 8am on Friday as McLaren had a "run plan" for FP1 I needed to be at before it began at 11am. I was testing various aero elements in the F1 session and couldn't really show my true pace with no "max" attack laps, but it was a good, fun session overall. It was about me doing consistent runs and giving the engineers good feedback to help them for the rest of the weekend. It was a fantastic experience to drive an F1 car around Spa.'

Norris went on to say how he only had 25 minutes between F1's FP1 and his F2 practice session and he had to cycle down to the F2 paddock to get ready quickly. As for the racing, he was placed fourth in the feature race as he was unable to find a way past Russell, who was placed third. However, some technical changes to his car's set-up did the trick the following day, and in the sprint race, Norris was second behind winner Nyck de Vries.

A week later, Norris was given another chance in FP1 at Monza, the home of the Italian Grand Prix; however, thunderstorms had made conditions extremely difficult, and he was limited to just nine laps, which he explained in the second half of his diary with Sky Sports.

'My second FP1 appearance was still fun despite the wet weather,' he wrote. 'It was short, just nine laps, but clean. McLaren needed to conserve tyre usage, but I was happy with my pace, initially on wets then [intermediate tyres], in the few laps I did.'

'I enjoy driving in the wet so a few more laps would have been cool. I still learned a lot comparing data with Fernando, for example. Of course I'd have liked more laps but being able to compare my times and data with Fernando is a pretty cool thing. Both cars were doing aero tests, for this year and next, and so the team, and myself, will have learned different things.

'With my F1 tests and doing FP1 at the last two Grands Prix it is making everything feel more natural for me. I don't feel as nervous, but it's still a big deal for me each time I walk into the McLaren pit box – it's pretty special. Every time I get in the McLaren, I feel more comfortable, my confidence increases and I feel more at home with the team.

'Hopefully the team sees that I've done OK this year and am worthy of a drive, having driven in different weather and adapting from high to low downforce. Hopefully there will be more opportunities to compete in FP1 at other GPs this year, but I'll just wait and see what happens.'

Lando had certainly impressed during the Monza practice session – despite finishing behind Alonso in the time sheets, the two drivers had traded places frequently in the difficult conditions.

Meanwhile, reaching the crunch end of the Formula 2 season, Norris was placed down in sixth in the Italian feature race and fifth in the sprint after two bad starts in the wet conditions, which cost him valuable points in the championship. Crucially, Russell, who had qualified on pole, won the sprint race, with Norris ending up off track when he tried an ambitious overtake on his title rival.

McLaren released the news that Norris would become their F1 driver for the 2019 season on 3 September 2018. It was not an unexpected appointment, for he had been patiently waiting for his opportunities in practice and had been impressive when doing so in his two recent opportunities. Furthermore, the team had already announced that Vandoorne would be leaving the team, with Zak Brown admitting he had never really been given a suitable race car with which to show his talent.

'We're immensely thankful for Stoffel's dedication, hard work and commitment during his time at McLaren,' he said in a press release. 'He's a talented racing driver with an incredible list of accolades in his junior career. We're proud to have played a part in his break into Formula One, from his role as test driver to his fantastic points-scoring debut in Bahrain in 2016. It's clear we haven't provided Stoffel with the tools to show his true talent, but throughout our relationship he's proved to be a fantastic team player. His work ethic is impressive, he has a great reputation within the team and we've really enjoyed working with him. Of course, we would have loved to achieve more success during our time together, but that doesn't detract from the fact that he will always be a part of the McLaren family of grand prix drivers. We wish Stoffel all the best in whatever direction he chooses to take next in his career, and we'll be supporting him all the way. We will announce our full driver line-up for the 2019 season in due course.'

The timing was telling, Vandoorne had only qualified in twentieth place for the Italian Grand Prix the previous weekend and Norris' name was one of three linked with replacing him, alongside Sergio Pérez, who had previously driven for the team in 2013 and was overdelivering with Racing Point. Frenchman Esteban Ocon was another name linked with the role, but the smart money was always on Norris, particularly due to his close links with Brown, who was overhauling the team.

Vandoorne was dignified in his exit, thanking the team before completing the season and moving to Formula E and eventually taking a position as a Mercedes reserve driver. But all eyes were now on McLaren – and there was not too long to wait before the official confirmation came that Norris had been hired as Vandoorne's replacement.

'McLaren is delighted to announce that Lando Norris will complete McLaren's driver line-up for the 2019 season,' said the team's PR release.

'Lando, eighteen, from Somerset, UK, is McLaren test and reserve driver and is contending the 2018 FIA Formula 2 Championship. He currently sits second in the championship, having won on his Formula 2 debut from pole position, with four races from two events remaining,' it stated. 'Lando will partner Spaniard Carlos Sainz, 24, at McLaren in 2019, as part of a multi-year agreement with the team. Although 2019 will be Lando's first season racing in Formula 1, he is no stranger to McLaren or F1 machinery. Lando has been part of the McLaren Young Driver Programme since early 2017, when he officially joined the team as test and simulator driver. Since then, Lando has regularly conducted race simulation work for the team and also participated in Formula 1 testing – in Abu Dhabi in 2017, and Spain and Hungary in 2018. Most recently, he has driven in the first free practice sessions in both Belgium and Italy.'

The key details were buried in the background information, which included the fact that this was a 'multi-year agreement' – an indication of just how highly Norris was rated by McLaren.

It is rare for a team to confirm the exact length of the contract; however, the 'multi-year agreement' made it clear that the young Brit was obviously central to Brown's long-term plan to help turn the struggling team around.

In the press release, Brown provided the following quote: 'We believe Lando is an exciting talent, full of potential, who we've very deliberately kept within the McLaren fold for exactly that reason. We already know he's fast, he learns quickly, and has a mature head on his young shoulders. We see much potential for our future together.

'The investment we have made in his budding career with simulator development and seat-time in the car has been well-deserved, as he has continued to prove his abilities both behind the wheel and in his work with the engineering team. Lando is an integral part of our plan for rebuilding our Formula 1 operation for the future, and he has already developed a strong relationship with the team.

'In Lando and Carlos we have an impressive duo who, despite their relative youth, hold valuable experience in Formula 1 and with McLaren, and represent the next generation of McLaren drivers to lead the team forward. While our short-term focus is fixed on securing the best possible result for the remainder of the 2018 season, we're also massively motivated by the opportunities that lie ahead.'

And what did Norris have to say about the new deal? He took to Twitter, saying it was a 'dream come true' and posted a childhood video of himself spinning around in a mini kart. 'If I could go back and tell this guy he'd be a McLaren F1 driver in 2019, he wouldn't believe me. Amazing opportunity. Dream come true,' he wrote.

A day later, McLaren called a press conference for a handful of journalists at the MTC. There would be the opportunity to speak to Norris and Brown about the deal they'd just struck.

I was due to attend and was on my way until my old Vespa PX200 decided to conk out on the A3 a few miles from Woking, so while I waited for it to cool down and after replacing the spark plug, I struck a deal with my colleagues that I'd transcribe the interview to make up for not actually making it there in time. The interview covered a lot of old ground, but Norris was more relaxed and honest when he was once again asked about the comparison with Lewis Hamilton.

'I did not grow up idolising Lewis,' he said, 'he was a driver who I admired, and you look at his characteristics and it is outright speed and outright pace, which is probably better than everyone else. My idol was MotoGP rider, Valentino Rossi. He was the first guy I started supporting when I was six or seven, but to be compared to Lewis in any way is still a cool thing.'

He was subsequently asked if he had celebrated his promotion to the pinnacle of motor sport by splashing some cash. He innocently revealed that the most expensive item he had bought with his race earnings so far was his airbrushing equipment that he used to paint his helmets.

'I've not bought anything,' he said. 'Instead of taking all the glory, I am just focusing on the job itself and if McLaren gives me a car, that's fine,' he added cheekily. 'I don't tend to buy fancy stuff anyway. I don't think I have ever spent over £1,000 on anything out of my own money. The most expensive thing I have ever bought is airbrush equipment for my painting. It sounds odd, but I like designing my own graphics and so having my own vinyl cutter, all the airbrushing equipment and paints all come up to a hefty price. I had it in my parent's house, in my room, which wasn't probably the best with all the chemicals, but I like to paint my own helmets, it is a pretty cool thing to do. I design my own suit and boots, I like being unique in that way. I used to take my helmets apart, sand them down and repaint. I think that's my favourite hobby after racing.'

Curiously, the conversation then switched to this education at Millfield School in Somerset where he'd left without any GCSEs, and he was asked about the naughtiest thing he had ever done while a student. Norris confessed to nicking a few penny sweets from the local shop – but that he then had to confess his crime to his mum. 'I haven't done much [naughty stuff]. I guess when I was five, it was not even bad, but I stole a sweet from the sweet shop. My parents found out and I lied and said they were given to us from school. Then my mum said she was going to ask the teacher, that's when I knew it was all going to go wrong, so I had to own up to it. Apart from that, nothing too naughty.'

Other revealing elements in the interview were the timeline for when he learned of McLaren's decision to promote him, which came in Italy after Vandoorne's poor result, plus how he would need to start getting in shape for the new season – despite his love of full-fat milk on his breakfast. 'I only found out on Sunday in Monza about the contract,' he said. 'I had to then keep it quiet until it was announced and then I got to tell everyone, including my mum. When she found out, she was crying. I think she's very proud. It has been a long time – eleven years of me travelling a lot and not seeing her, so to know that I've now got to where I wanted to be, I think she was very happy.'

And the change of diet and getting in his best shape? 'My trainer lives opposite me and comes and checks on me,' he explained. 'I should do better, but I have my Weetabix, I've had that pretty much all my life. I am probably the main consumer of Weetabix in the world, cold milk, full fat, but they are pretty strict. I think Weetabix and full-fat milk is what it is all about.'

Unsurprisingly, with such a wide-ranging interview, the news that Norris had finally got his shot in F1 received extensive coverage in the press. *The Times* explained how Norris was happy to remain near Guildford, with Rebecca Clancy writing that he would continue to rent a flat in Surrey with Sacha Fenestraz. 'It is not hard to see why Monaco draws in the top athletes,' she wrote, 'the glitz, glamour and weather, not to mention the beneficial tax system. The majority of Formula One drivers consider it home, but Lando Norris has no plans on joining them when he races for McLaren next season.'

The *Daily Mail*'s Jonathan McEvoy took a similar approach, writing: 'Have you heard about the grand prix driver who shares a flat to save on the bills? Or about the multi-millionaire's son whose most expensive gift to himself is an airbrush for which he saved up? Meet Lando Norris, who arrived as a confirmed Formula One racer with only a few pennies to rub together at the start of a career that could make him as rich as Croesus. While Lewis Hamilton will bank £40 million a year on his new Mercedes contract, the eighteen-year-old has agreed a three-season deal with McLaren worth £500,000 annually. Hardly a pittance, but not enough to prompt him to rush straight out for Monaco real estate brochures.' As for my piece for the *Sun* – the headline summed it up nicely: 'Monaco, parties & fizz? I like Guildford, painting & Weetabix.'

Elsewhere, Sky Sports noted that 'even when urging patience next season with the teenager, McLaren boss Zak Brown couldn't disguise his enthusiasm for a driver who has excelled in every series of his nascent career to date', adding 'the weakness of Norris' candidature is his age – especially when tallied with the 24-year-old Carlos Sainz. But Brown says the line-up – likely to be the youngest on the grid next season – is the right fit for McLaren's current position.' The website also explained how Norris had played down his role in helping turn the team's fortunes around, stating: 'We are not going to be winning, or competing against Ferrari and Mercedes. I would like to think we can make a step forward from where we are. McLaren need a fresh start and as a team we need two young drivers who are willing to say "we don't need to win within two years of joining the team". I think that's realistic. But we are not going to be winning next year and probably the year after. It's going to be a few years before we get back to where we want to be.'

Norris had aced his media commitments. Despite Brown's gushing praise, Norris had been truthful, provided honest anecdotes and been an engaging interviewee, but he had also been clear that he should not be portrayed as McLaren's saviour – nor the 'new Lewis Hamilton'.

Norris was quickly thrust into the public eye as many people were keen to learn more about this latest F1 rising star. But his focus was always on closing out the F2 season. He had held the lead in the championship until the sixth round in Austria when he was replaced at the top of the standings by Russell; however, he was still consistently scoring points and remained very much in the race for the title alongside Russell and Albon.

With four races remaining, Norris arrived in Russia in a confident mood ahead of the feature and sprint races. The circuit is situated in the Black Sea resort of Sochi and the track winds around venues used for ice hockey, speed skating, curling and figure skating at the 2014 Winter Olympic Games. Despite being under the spotlight, Norris topped the time sheets for the F2 practice session, while Russell made a mistake on his best flying lap, running off track. Norris had again been doubling up and had taken part in Friday's F1 FP1 session ahead of his run in F2 and headed the session from de Vries, who was second and Russell was third.

The following day, Norris kept up the pace and qualified in second place behind de Vries but crucially ahead of championship-leader Russell, who led for much of the qualifying session. De Vries' late lap clinched pole, denying Norris the four bonus points that meant that Russell still had a 22-point lead going into the feature race.

Unfortunately, that was as good as the weekend got for Norris as his chances of winning the title were completely wiped out with a double retirement in both the feature and sprint races.

In the feature race, Norris made a poor start from second place and quickly dropped down the order. Panicking, he made a rare mistake on his pit stop, first missing his slot and then hastily pulling away too quickly without his front-right tyre properly attached, ultimately leading to him retiring the car. The race was won by Albon, while Russell took fourth and extended his lead over Norris to 34 points.

The sprint race was even worse, applying the final axe to any hopes Norris had of challenging Russell for the title. He had progressed from eighteenth to twelfth place until he received a stop-go penalty for crossing the safety car line on the formation lap. He was then hit by Arjun Maini and retired with a puncture. Meanwhile, Russell won the race and set the fastest lap to move 37 points above Albon, who was now in second place in the championship.

Writing his F2 diary for Sky Sports, Norris wrote: 'So guys, this will be a short one … there's not a huge amount to say, and there's certainly no "from Russia with love" message here after what can only be summed up as a horrendous weekend on my Sochi debut. I'll be heading to the final F2 event in Abu Dhabi next month in "max attack" mode. The championship title has gone after suffering my first non-finishes of the season. So I'll just have some fun in Abu Dhabi and try and get P2 in the standings. I'll do my very best, I won't give up, and I'll work together with Carlin to achieve the best results and hopefully finish the year off with a couple of wins.'

At the final grand prix of the year, Norris honoured his promise and finished fifth in the feature race after qualifying in seventh. In the sprint race, he was second behind Antonio Fuoco. That, along with Albon finishing in fourteenth and eighth in the two races, ensured Norris had accumulated enough points for second place in the championship behind Russell, who was crowned champion, much to Norris' frustration.

THE LITTLE BROTHER

As the clock ticked down to the opening race of the 2019 Formula One season, it was inevitable that the spotlight would fall on McLaren and their driver pairing of Norris and Sainz. Norris was very much Zak Brown's boy, he'd asserted himself in the team and there was a distinct feeling that he would be the future of McLaren.

Sainz had arrived from Renault where he had been replaced by Daniel Ricciardo, while Renault had kept faith in Nico Hulkenberg as their other driver. It was disappointing for Sainz to lose his seat as he had not fared too badly in the previous season, finishing tenth place in the championship. But the bigger change surrounding his move to McLaren was that he would cut his ties to Red Bull, who had masterminded his career since 2010 when he was competing in the BMW Formula Europe championship.

McLaren confirmed his position in the team in April 2018, well in advance of announcing Norris in September. McLaren had been weighing up whether to go with Sainz or Ricciardo from Red Bull. The Aussie would later replace the Spaniard at McLaren.

Sainz was billed as the replacement for countryman Fernando Alonso, who had announced that he was retiring from the sport.

Parallels were drawn between the two, with Sainz agreeing a two-year deal, marking 'the next chapter' in his career.

In the press release, he spoke about 'being a McLaren fan for as long as I can remember', adding: 'It's a great name in the sport with an incredible heritage, and the list of drivers that have raced for McLaren over the years are among the heroes of Formula One. Fernando is of course one of them, so it's particularly special that I'll be taking his seat as part of the next generation of Spanish racing drivers behind the wheel of a McLaren.'

Heading into the new season, it was interesting to see how the relationship between Sainz and Norris would develop. Team rivalry is an intriguing dynamic in F1 racing – while teammates remain opponents on the track, a level of cooperation between them is vital for ensuring that the team makes progress.

A positive partnership between Norris and Sainz would be crucial for McLaren's new era and the revival of their fortunes after an extended period of underwhelming results that stretched back to the 2012 season when Hamilton and Button were behind the wheel.

For Norris, he would need to hold his own against an experienced racer in Sainz, but it was obvious that he had been prepped for his debut in F1 for a number of years.

'I had been working with Lando for quite some time since I had first met him,' explains Charlotte Sefton, who initially looked after Sainz's media commitments in F1. 'He was at the McLaren Technology Centre a lot through his time with the Young Driver Programme, and because he lived in Guilford at the time, he was being asked to come into the factory more than any of the other drivers, especially more than Fernando, Jenson or Stoffel. He would do the media commitments the others did not want to do, or couldn't do, as they did not live in the UK, so we spent quite a bit of time together, even though I was due to look after Carlos.

'But what I would also say is that from day one, his trainer John and manager Mark had made it clear that we should in no way mollycoddle him. They told me not to give him any leeway when it comes to being late. They actually asked me to inform them if Lando was late or something was out of line because they wanted to mould him into a professional racing driver, so that he could be relied upon and always had the right approach.

'If he turned up late, I had to tell them and explain it. Of course, there was the other side of it. We would go down to the pit lane and celebrate when he was on the podium, and he'd just be really chuffed to think that people had come out to support him. We kind of knew that he was on this path.'

While Norris was still very much a rookie, Sainz was about to embark on his fifth season in F1 with his third team, and the Spaniard's experience obviously had an effect on the relationship between him and Norris.

'I was lucky to see the dynamic between the two of them from the beginning,' Sefton says. 'Carlos had come to the team with this attitude of, "I've been in F1 for five years, I've got loads of experience, I am going to be the team's number one driver." He saw this as his opportunity to step out of the shadows of his teammate, and because he'd left the Red Bull family, he was going it alone. As a result, he spoke to Lando like a little brother.' I was not alone in wondering how this was all going to go.

'We'd obviously been told that we had to keep Lando on the straight and narrow and he was forever trying to rebel by not wearing the right thing. He'd turn up not in team trainers or have something on that was not team issue. He was trying to test us, and I was like, "How come Carlos is always on time and looked the part?" He once asked me why I was always telling him about Carlos, and I told him to come back to me once he'd done five years in F1. I had taken on this big sister role, so by the time I did start working with him, we already had a good relationship. Sometimes I'd just go and sit with him in his driver's room and chat about life.'

Formula One's off-season is a peculiar time as it marks the busiest period for the majority of the team – but not the drivers. Car designs are refined, wind-tunnel time is at a premium and it is all hands to the pump when it comes to ensuring that the car the team has at the season-opener is the quickest it can be. It requires plenty of long nights for the staff, who are constantly assessing the data. However, even if internal targets are hit, no team is really sure how they will stack up against the opposition. The first real test comes in the qualifying session for the opening race of the season.

Nonetheless, as a rookie, Norris did have plenty to work on, particularly his fitness. At nineteen, he was still scrawny, and it was evident that he would struggle with the effects of his first long runs in an F1 car. Building up neck muscles is imperative for a driver to withstand regular g-forces of six times their body weight. His diet was also improved to become more balanced, although there had already been some progress on this front in the form of meals being specially prepared for him to cook at home.

Norris and Sainz were present at the team's lavish launch of their MCL34 car at the MTC in Woking in February. In the media questions that followed, Norris was made aware that at nineteen, he would become the youngest British driver to compete in Formula One, and in response, he honestly admitted that he would inevitably make some errors in his first season.

'There's going to be times when I make mistakes but it's just knowing that's part of it,' he said to a group of selected journalists. 'No one's perfect. I'm sure there's going to be times when I do things wrong that no one's going to like and everyone's going to think I'm terrible and rubbish, but I know I'm going to get through those times. It's just understanding that that's going to happen. It's very different when you get to F1 knowing when I make one small mistake a lot more people are going to see it. There's more pressure in knowing you're under more scrutiny.

'I've spent a lot of time over the winter to try and prepare myself in every way for this moment and for the races, but there's some things you can't learn until you're on track and in that situation. The aim is to win races and championships, but we have to improve as a team first.'

McLaren had been under-delivering for years, despite having talents such as Fernando Alonso and Jenson Button as drivers. Norris had seen first-hand the former's abilities when they competed as teammates in the Daytona 24 Hours the previous year, although they finished a disappointing eighth for Zak Brown's United Autosports team.

Brown was also keen to play down his team's chances for 2019. Instead, he stressed how McLaren were undergoing a rebuilding process. Tim Goss had left his role as technical director and Matt Morris had resigned from his position as chief engineer. Pat Fry temporarily returned to the team as engineering director having previously worked for McLaren between 1993 and 2010 before moving to Ferrari. They had also recruited James Key as technical director from Scuderia Toro Rosso. Andreas Seidl, who had been in charge of Porsche's highly successful world endurance championship team, would also be joining in May as managing director. Peter Prodromou, who rejoined McLaren in 2017 from Red Bull Racing and worked alongside Adrian Newey, continued in his role of chief aerodynamics engineer, despite some inherent problems with the previous year's challenger. Nonetheless, there were some encouraging signs and the Renault engine was definitely an improvement on the previous Honda power units. However, Brown was cautious with saddling his two new drivers, especially Norris, with the burden of carrying the team, particularly in the absence of Alonso, who had extracted the maximum from the car the previous season to help the team finish sixth in the constructors' standings.

'Lando is very mature for his age and has been in a race car for most of his life,' said Brown at the car launch. 'He is a relaxed individual and we think he is ready otherwise we would not put him in the car. I am sure he will make some rookie mistakes but we will be there to support him. I think he will hit the ground running and will be on it right away.'

And that is exactly what did happen during the winter test in Barcelona in February. Preseason testing is a crucial precursor to the season where teams get to run their new cars to check for performance and faults, while also monitoring what their opponents are doing. Teams even employ 'spy photographers' in the pit lane, who shoot each car leaving the garages, and the pictures are then relayed back to HQ for forensic assessment by the technical departments. In the pit lane, teams use screens to hide away all their hard work, especially when it comes to cars running the bright flow-vis paint that produces patterns replicating airflow over bodywork.

It is an exciting time for teams, drivers, journalists and fans following the winter break, and it offers a fresh chance to reassess driver pairings and prospects for the upcoming season. Just one car from each team is used (to control costs – crucial in the budget-cap era) which allows the smaller teams to have the same amount of running time as the bigger ones. There is, of course, no limit on how many laps a team can do within the 9am–6pm testing window. Sometimes, cars look quick, but other times, there is clearly some sandbagging – as teams attempt to make their cars look slower than they are to avoid extra scrutiny.

But there was no hiding for Norris after he neared the top of the time sheets on his first day as a Formula One driver on 19 February on the second day of the first test in Spain. Sainz had been given the drive on the opening day, and he notched up nearly 120 laps and had a virtually trouble-free day. Norris' run, however, went even better as the Brit powered his McLaren to the top of the testing charts. He finished the day second-quickest and just three tenths of a second off Ferrari's Charles Leclerc. It was a vast improvement for the team given Alonso's first day of testing the previous year where a wheel had literally fallen off his McLaren and they were hampered by overheating issues. 'It is an improvement,' Norris told the media after his time behind the wheel. 'It's good confidence for myself and the team. It is good to know we can get through pretty much a whole day with no big problems.'

The team concluded their eight days of winter testing and left quietly confident, mainly due to the lack of drama. For once, they had completed a normal preseason programme, which in the previous years had been dominated by power unit failures and poor reliability. McLaren left Spain with plenty of data to analyse, while Brown continued to talk about a 'new chapter' with them facing a 'long road ahead'. Nonetheless, the American must have been pleased with his team's performance as he headed for Josep Tarradellas Barcelona–El Prat airport.

The Australian Grand Prix is the perfect curtain-raiser for a new Formula One season. It is a long way to travel for European-based teams, but there is always something special about arriving in Melbourne for the opening race. I caught up with both Lando and George Russell before catching my flight to Australia and asked them a series of quick-fire questions, and looking back at the pair's responses, it is clear just how young both drivers were, especially Norris:

Who was your boyhood hero?
George Russell: 'Michael Schumacher'
Lando Norris: 'Valentino Rossi'

Who was your favourite F1 driver when you were a kid?
GR: 'Juan Pablo Montoya'
LN: 'Lewis Hamilton'
What are your three favourite possessions?
GR: 'Friends, family and girlfriend.'
LN: 'Simulator, my headphones and privacy.'

What are your hobbies outside of F1?
GR: 'I enjoy playing a bit of squash.'
LN: 'Sim racing and graphic design. I like painting my crash helmets.'

If you were hosting a dinner party and you could invite three guests, dead or alive, who would you pick?
GR: 'Sir Frank Williams, Jennifer Aniston and James Hunt.'
LN: 'Daniel Ricciardo, Zak Brown and Valentino Rossi.'

What's your favourite film?
GR: '*Casino Royale.*'
LN: '*Austin Powers*, the second one with Mini Me.'

What's your favourite band?
GR: 'I don't really have one. I don't have a stand-out artist. If I had to pick one, I'd say Justin Timberlake.'
LN: 'I don't have one. If I had to pick a type of music, it would be the chill-out albums.'

What was your first car?
GR: 'VW Polo'
LN: 'Mini Cooper D'

Current car?
GR: 'Mercedes C63'
LN: 'VW Polo'

What would be your ideal date night?
GR: 'Dinner in a nice restaurant with a great view. Maybe a glass of champagne and some nice food.'
LN: 'I'd ask her what she wants to do!'

What's your favourite food to eat?
GR: 'Pizza'
LN: 'Chicken katsu curry'

If you have £10 left in your wallet, what would you buy?
GR: 'I would invest in somewhere to make more money.'
LN: 'I would go to the casino!'

Norris linked up with the rest of the 60-strong McLaren team on 11 March following some extra time factored in to allow him to acclimatise to the time difference. Sleep is one of the fundamental things to crack when travelling Down Under as Melbourne is eleven hours ahead of the UK. Many teams are still trying to find out the best way to combat the effects of jet lag. Some teams encourage their staff to start shifting their sleep patterns in the days running up to departure. Some suggest the use of sleeping tablets and the wearing of sunglasses to limit sun exposure. Maintaining good nutrition and exercise is also crucial for drivers.

McLaren have had a long partnership with the Hilton hotel chain that continued into 2019 as the team took up residence in the centre of town, with the Albert Park track just a short drive away. The set-up crew normally arrives at the track ten days before the race to prepare the garage and unload the twelve tonnes of sea freight that leaves the UK in early January. Heavy equipment, such as the garage signage, work benches, generators and pit-stop apparatus, is sent via container ships to reduce freight costs. Incredibly, McLaren has five sets of racing freight travelling around the world at any one time as they pass from one race to another. After Melbourne, the equipment would then head to Montreal for the Canadian GP. During European races, the equipment is usually sent via a fleet of trucks, and the 28 tonnes of car-related parts are usually the last to arrive at the track.

While his teammates cracked on with building his garage, Lando's car was prepared under the watchful eye of his race engineer, Will Joseph. The Cambridge graduate was previously the race team performance engineer and had worked with Alonso, Kevin Magnussen, Sergio Pérez and Lewis Hamilton, ensuring their cars were optimised for racing conditions. Joseph made sure Lando's car was ready to go before the FIA's strict curfew came into operation, which requires all engineers and mechanics to check out of the paddock to give them a break. Ahead of the race, Norris' responsibilities mainly involved media and sponsorship appearances, but he would also take a track walk to assess the condition of the Albert Park circuit and get a real-world perspective after putting in hours and hours of work on the simulator.

Given there are 17,000 kilometres between McLaren's Woking HQ and Melbourne's Albert Park, the simulator work that Norris had done was the only real preparation that could assist him in the build up to his F1 debut. Before the event, Lando explained that he had driven the track around 600 times. As well as the team's simulator, he had his own hi-tech set-up in his flat in Guildford, which included a Pro-Sim Evolution simulator that cost around £30,000 and sat pride of place in his living room.

'In terms of laps of Albert Park,' he said, 'I must have done 600 or something. I have a decent understanding. You get to a point where you can do so much on the simulator, but then it always changes when you get to the track and you get to drive it for real for the first time.'

But had all the extra practice at home helped him in terms of confidence ahead of his F1 debut? He appeared relaxed in the paddock, and he was also on good form when he took the stage on the Wednesday at Melbourne's Federation Square as it hosted a season launch event for the first time. He was obviously doing a great job of hiding his nerves as after all he was just a few hours away from fulfilling his ambition of racing an F1 car in a grand prix.

'He was so nervous,' admits Sefton. 'You could tell because he just went very, very quiet. Like steely quiet. He was not like a rabbit in the headlights because he had been prepared. He texted me saying he did not want to muck up, and I just said to him, "You have nothing to lose. There's no expectations on you. You've just got to go out there and the one thing we can say is, don't crash. Anything else is a bonus. This is just about experience, you're putting a lot of pressure on yourself." I actually remember him coming into the track on Sunday and he told me he had not slept because he was just so wired. He was really quiet. It was almost like he wasn't in the room. We decided just to leave him alone and let him do his own thing. I had already told him that we would not be doing a lot of media to reduce the pressure, but he is always the hardest person on himself. I just tried to reassure him that he was doing an amazing job for the team and that he should be proud of himself and that his family, who were there, were just so happy for him.'

Ahead of the race, the *Daily Mail* run an article featuring Norris and Russell as they both prepared to make their F1 debuts. Russell was driving for the Williams team, effectively on loan from Mercedes; however, he knew that his chances of impressing had been hampered by the team's failure to take part in much of the dedicated testing days as their car was simply not ready in time. The *Mail* hailed Lando and George's arrival in F1 as 'the most exciting newcomers produced in this country since [Hamilton] made his scintillating debut on the same tarmac twelve years [earlier]'.

Friday's practice was overshadowed by the sudden death of FIA race director Charlie Whiting, who was a legend of the sport. He joined the Hesketh Racing team in 1977, but following the team's collapse, he went to Bernie Ecclestone's Brabham team, working his way up to become chief mechanic for Nelson Piquet's world title wins in 1981 and 1983. He joined the FIA in 1998 as technical delegate to Formula One and was appointed FIA director and safety delegate in 1997. His openness and honesty made him popular with the drivers, and the sport was plunged into mourning following his passing.

Whiting was replaced by Australian Michael Masi, who would hold the role until the end of the 2021 season. Masi's availability in Melbourne meant that the Australian GP was still able to go ahead, and on Friday 15 March, Lando Norris took part in his first session as a full-time F1 driver. He may have driven the track on McLaren's simulator and on his own gaming rig countless times, but he notched up 31 real laps in first practice – more than any other driver. Working his way through a series of tests and training programmes, his lap times were unsurprisingly slow, and he finished the session in eighteenth on the time sheets.

Second practice saw Lando record another eighteenth-placed spot. And it was a hat-trick of P18s after final practice, following a session that also saw Norris hauled in front of the stewards to provide an explanation as to why he was released from his garage and into the path of Williams' Robert Kubica. It was an unfortunate accident that was not Lando's fault, for he was unaware of the Polish driver's location, but such incidents are potentially dangerous, and the FIA deals with them harshly. Rather like a naughty schoolboy, Lando was told to recount what had happened to the stewards, and once they'd listened to his explanation, they issued a €5,000 fine to McLaren for an unsafe release.

Somehow, this brush with the officials seemed to give Norris some added impetus and he appeared to have the bit between his teeth when it came to qualifying. He had looked accomplished and consistent in his three practices, if a little unspectacular. But just as he had done in F2 in Bahrain on his debut, he announced his arrival in F1 with aplomb on Saturday afternoon's opening qualifying session.

The hour-long session is split into three segments as drivers set their best lap times to make the cut to reach the top-ten shootout. Norris had looked set for an early exit in Q1. His previous outings in all three practice sessions had given the impression that he was nailed on for another eighteenth place. So, when he eventually finished up in eighth place on the grid, it was a genuine surprise to everyone. He outqualified former world champion Kimi Räikkönen and Sergio Pérez. He was also higher up the grid than his more experienced teammate as Sainz was eliminated in Q1 and would be lining up in eighteenth place on the grid for Sunday's race. The Spaniard was unhappy and blamed Kubica's crash for forcing him to slow down on his qualifying lap. Unsurprisingly, 2018 world champion Hamilton took pole with Valtteri Bottas clinching second and Vettel in third.

The first race of the year is always a special occasion. The Albert Park track is popular with the drivers and the local fans, who create a great atmosphere. There was particular excitement for the 2019 season with the arrival of the two new British drivers on the grid, in addition to Alex Albon getting his chance with Toro Rosso. The season also saw the Alfa Romeo brand come back to F1 and the launch of Racing Point, formerly Force India.

There was a genuine feel-good factor around the circuit as Hamilton looked to defend his world crown in the season opener – but could any other driver on the grid take the fight to him?

As for Norris, he was unable to capitalise on his eighth-place start and eventually came home twelfth after making a few errors. 'The team gave me a good car, with enough pace for me to be in the top ten,' he said afterwards, 'but I made a couple of mistakes which cost me any chance of scoring points, so I'm a little disappointed. But it's cool to finish my first F1 race and get it out of the way. I didn't make the perfect start, struggled to get ahead of a slower car and then had a big lock-up so I need to work on these mistakes. I'm annoyed with myself as there was more potential.'

Typically hard on himself, this was an incredible achievement on his first GP and in an uncompetitive car, but Norris was unhappy to finish outside the points, which is a harsh assessment when you consider the fruitless years McLaren had had from 2013 onwards. Such was the pressure Lando had put on himself, he actually decided to apologise to the team for failing to score points, even though he did not need to make any such apology. 'I'm a bit annoyed because there was a lot more potential,' he reflected. 'The car had the pace to be in the top ten. Basically I let everyone down so I need to make sure that doesn't happen again. The possibility was there; to finish in the points was there. I just made a couple of mistakes that put me outside of it, which is why I'm not as happy as I was on Saturday.'

While Norris was being incredibly self-critical, his teammate Sainz was left reflecting on a disappointing start to his McLaren career. His debut for the team was cut short after ten laps when he was forced to retire with an engine problem. Meanwhile, Norris' rival Russell had a trouble-free race but could only manage sixteenth.

A NEW DEAL

Two weeks after Australia, at the Bahrain Grand Prix, Norris would get his first points on the board. At a track where he had previous experience and had achieved some success, he was able to start his weekend on the front foot. He notched a fifteenth place in first practice and then went even better in the Friday afternoon session to finish eighth. He started his Saturday with a seventh in final practice before again defying the odds to make it into Q3 and qualify in tenth place. He was moved up to ninth on the grid for Sunday owing to a penalty for Romain Grosjean, who was demoted from eighth to eleventh.

Norris took full advantage in the race to come home in sixth place, sandwiched between two world champions; just behind Vettel's Ferrari and in front of Räikkönen's Alfa Romeo. 'I'm really happy and pleased to have scored my first points but also for McLaren after all of the team's hard work over the winter,' he said after the race. 'I had a good start: a good launch, good pull away but then some wheelspin. I was blocked going into Turn One, then was on the outside of another car and we touched. I went off and through the gravel, losing quite a few places but the pace after that was really strong. I caught up pretty quickly. I maybe struggled a little in the final stint but managed to stay ahead of Kimi.' It was a much-needed boost to the team, especially as Sainz was again forced to retire with a gearbox problem. Norris had outraced and outperformed his more experienced teammate in the opening two races and had been in a position to benefit from the two Renaults retiring in the final three laps. Understandably, when we spoke post-race, he was suitably pleased. 'It feels good,' he said. 'We got a bit lucky with the Renaults. I was under a bit of pressure from Kimi, but we finally got rewarded with what we deserved as a team. Between qualifying and the race, it has been our strongest for quite some time. There is still a lot of work to do but our race pace was better than anticipated. For my first two races of the season, although Australia could have been better, I have made up for it here.'

Despite his success, there was no room for any wild partying, and he insisted that he'd be having a quiet one to toast his first points as an F1 driver. 'I won't be drinking,' he said when asked how he would celebrate the landmark. 'I want to stay away from that stuff this year. This is my chance to do well, and this is my career ahead of me and I don't want to do anything stupid. Things can happen when you drink too much. I will celebrate and be with the guys though. It's great getting another race, with more attacking and defending, gaining experience in quite a few areas, which I couldn't do in Australia because you can't overtake. It gives me more confidence for the next race. I will be able to react quicker and make more of my own decisions. I am moving forward.'

Unfortunately, Norris did not have much of a chance to use his growing sense of confidence and suffered a disappointing end to the Chinese Grand Prix, which followed two weeks later. He had qualified in fifteenth place, one slot behind Sainz, but both were hit by Toro Rosso's Daniil Kvyat on the opening lap. The Russian clipped the front wing of Sainz's McLaren and launched him into Norris, catapulting the Brit into the air.

While all three drivers were initially able to carry on, Norris and Kvyat were eventually forced to retire from the race, and Sainz eventually finished fourteenth.

Kvyat was hit with a drive-through penalty for causing the accident – one of the harshest penalties available to the stewards – that results in a driver coming into the pits and stopping for ten seconds before his team are even allowed to start working on his car. He is then sent back out on track again, having lost all the time in the pit stop, plus the extra ten seconds. In what was hardly a shock, Kvyat was upset with the decision. In his post-race comments, he told Sky Sports: 'I totally disagree with the penalty and I will speak to the stewards behind closed doors to find out their opinion. It was a corner exit and my car was already totally straight. The regulation says I need to leave a car's width to the car next to me. It was three cars in one corner and one car coming back on track very sharply. The other car was sandwiched and then I went in the air from a car which hit me from behind and then I went into Norris' car. I've seen my on-board and Lando's on-board. Honestly, I don't see this incident as very particular, it was a typical lap-one sandwich. These things happen, especially on lap one so I don't really understand [the penalty].'

As with such incidents in F1, there is always a counter-argument, and Sainz offered his own perspective, blaming his former Toro Rosso teammate, suggesting he needed to be more patient on the opening lap in Shanghai. 'It is Lap One, obviously I understand his frustrations [at the penalty] and it can happen,' he said. 'It is Lap One and there are 55 laps to go, so if you don't get the best of starts … look at your teammate who has finished in the points starting from the pit lane. It is a long race and you don't have to open the steering wheel on the exit of a corner when you know you have two McLarens side-by-side. It's a long race, you can overtake even if you don't have the best of starts. You have to be patient and think that you can get back into the points. That's exactly what Lando and I were doing and we were in a bit of a melee.'

The up-and-down nature of the season continued in the fourth race in Azerbaijan. All eyes were on Hamilton as he opened up a lead at the top of the championship, but for McLaren, the race in Baku marked a key moment for the team as they secured a double-points finish. Both Norris and Sainz reached the final stage of qualifying to start inside the top ten. And they converted that with Sainz in seventh and Norris eighth. The haul of ten points also helped McLaren climb to fourth place in the constructors' championship.

Before the next race in Spain, Norris received a justified and timely upgrade in the form of a new company car – a £150,000 McLaren 570s in papaya orange that would replace his VW Polo. Arranging the insurance proved to be particularly problematic given that he was only nineteen at the time and had only held a UK driving licence for two years. In Barcelona, I asked him how it felt to be given such a dream car at his age. 'I only got it last week. I haven't driven it that much,' he told me. 'Instead of going to get food from a local shop, which is a ten-second walk outside my door, I went to a supermarket, which is a couple of miles away. I made the effort to have a drive, which was quite nice. I had the roof down and had a nice drive. I didn't drive it that much and I didn't drive it fast. I've got a job I need to keep, so I can't be that stupid!'

I also took the opportunity to find out how the home cooking was going – and the laundry. 'I have ready-to-cook meals,' he said. 'I just throw it in the microwave. My nutritionist sorts it all out. There is a company who drops it off. I just keep it in the freezer and then put it in the oven. It's much safer than cooking. I don't really do my washing either. When I went to see my parents last week, instead of doing laundry at my place, I took a whole bag back to do it there.' Once again, a refreshingly honest and light-hearted response from McLaren's rising star.

But there was no laughing when Norris and Lance Stroll collided 22 laps from the end of the Spanish GP, while battling for fourteenth place. Both ended up spinning off and damaging their cars. Norris did manage to get his McLaren moving, but only for a few metres before he was forced to admit defeat. He radioed his team, saying, 'I'm sorry, guys, I am out.' It was disappointing for Norris, who had started the race in tenth place after another excellent qualifying, even if he believed Stroll, the Canadian son of billionaire Lawrence Stroll, who was bankrolling the Racing Point team, had been at fault. But it was Norris' second failure to finish in the opening five races, and he needed to be careful to avoid gaining a negative reputation.

As a result, he was reserved in his criticism after the race in the paddock, saying, 'I haven't heard what he thought and what he knew about the incident. I just know I had my car on the inside for Turn Two, having been on the outside for Turn One. He left me space for Turn One so he knew I was there. I don't know if he thought I had disappeared, but he then just cut across the front of my car and took us both out. I let the team down because I didn't finish the race so I said sorry to my guys, definitely not to him [Stroll].' While the stewards did not punish either racer, Norris would not be drawn into a mud-slinging contest and added: 'This was my first time on track against him so I don't want to comment on that. He didn't leave me enough room today and I'll leave it at that.'

After Barcelona, the next race was Monaco. The Monte Carlo showpiece is always a fantastic event, but in 2019, it was all rather subdued. On 20 May, less than a week before the race, Niki Lauda passed away. The Austrian was a three-time F1 world champion and non-executive chairman of the Mercedes team. Lauda was a larger-than-life character who had defied the odds to return to racing following a fiery smash at the Nürburgring in 1976 when he was fighting James Hunt for the world championship. He made an astonishing return to racing just six weeks after his accident, finishing fourth in Monza despite his weeping wounds being heavily bandaged up. In Monaco, teams paid their respects, while Mercedes painted their halos red and included a red three-pointed star on the engine cover on their cars as a nod to Lauda's distinctive red crash helmet and red cap that he would wear.

The race offered another chance for the media to ask Norris if he was planning on moving to Monaco now he was a fully fledged F1 driver. Hamilton was living there, Button did too during much of his F1 career. Other British racers still live there, including Paul di Resta and David Coulthard, but Norris was not interested. He had just started playing golf and said he would miss the countryside, and his mates, too much to move away from the UK just yet. In plain terms, he was also simply not earning enough to justify moving, and at this stage of his fledgling career, he knew it made sense for him to remain close to the team's factory in Woking.

When asked about the lure of Monaco, while sitting in the McLaren motorhome overlooking the principality's famous harbour and multimillion-dollar yachts, Norris was characteristically honest: 'In terms of the environment, it's not something which gets me excited or something I necessarily look forward to. None of my friends are here, so I won't know any people, it's just not as open and free as where I live now in Guildford. I can go to McLaren, I can go to do a lot more things with my mates, I can have more fun. Here I don't know what I should do.' He was still living a sheltered life. One weekend he was an F1 driver, the next he'd spend hours at home playing on his computer, barely leaving the house. 'I don't really have any school friends,' he added, 'it's just people from racing who are my friends now. Going out to play Top Golf the other day, which I've done once before, I'm not any good at golf, but I can just go and have some fun, and that's probably something I can't necessarily do here in Monaco. It's just being able to travel and do what I like doing. I don't think I would be able to do as many of those things here.'

Would a lucrative new contract change his mind, though? 'Then I would consider it,' he admitted, 'but I'm far from earning £30 million a year now. But I doubt the other drivers would move here unless it saved them enough money. I think that's pretty much the biggest talking point about it all. Rather than going, "I just want to move to Monaco because of the lifestyle and everything else." I am not surprised that people live here, a lot of the drivers here earn a decent amount of money and that's the benefit of being here.'

As for the race itself, Hamilton took the win while Norris was out of the points, down in eleventh place, moving up one spot on the grid from where he started. Sainz, who qualified in ninth, finished sixth, earning some good points in the process.

The up-and-down nature of Norris' season continued at the following race in Canada. He again impressed in qualifying, reaching the top eight, one place above Sainz. There were signs that McLaren were making good progress with their new driver line-up and the team were confident about taking a solid haul of points from the race in Montreal. But disaster struck for Norris in the most unlikeliest of ways eight laps in. He lost control of his McLaren when his rear-right suspension collapsed, forcing him out of the race. It later turned out that his brakes had been running so hot they had overheated and caught fire, causing the suspension to melt. It resulted in another DNF.

Despite the setbacks, the world – and more importantly McLaren – had seen enough from their young driver to persuade them that he was indeed a star of the future. In the aces he had finished, he had demonstrated that he had the racecraft required but also the temperament for when things did go wrong. He was a team player, and if McLaren were going to get out of the rut they had found themselves in since 2013, they required team players – rather than individuals.

It was around this time of the season that other teams were checking in on his availability too. His contract at McLaren was due to expire in December 2019, and it was not an especially lucrative one for an F1 driver – estimated to be worth around £380,000 a year – and it was unsurprising that the likes of Red Bull Racing were reprising their interest in Norris. The paddock gossip spread like wildfire, but Norris was clearly happy where he was. He had formed an excellent relationship with Zak Brown, and his team. He was also getting on with his teammate, who was not exactly destroying him in the championship, as had been the expectation.

So, ahead of the French Grand Prix in June, I raised the contract question and asked whether he was already looking to move teams and secure a bumper new contract. Normally, you can expect vague answers from drivers whenever contracts are mentioned, but Norris was forthright and said he wanted his future resolved as quickly as possible and ideally before the upcoming British Grand Prix at Silverstone. 'It would be nice if I could get it [the new deal] done and know I would be here for so many years. I am happy here at McLaren. I know everyone and the plan they have for the next few years, it is all looking a lot more positive and changes have been made for the better. I am happy. I am not saying I wouldn't enjoy it as much in other teams, but it is nice and relaxed, and I have a good teammate. It is chilled and a nice environment to be in right now. I can't just cruise around and have fun. I still have to do well. If a driver doesn't do well enough, they can always get cut but everything has been going to plan so far.'

Norris delivered his message for McLaren loud and clear. He wanted to stay. And he then left the team in no doubt about his talent as he pulled off his best qualifying performance in his F1 career to start the French GP in fifth place. He out-qualified Ferrari's Vettel and Red Bull's Pierre Gasly with a superb display at Paul Ricard. 'I'm happy,' he said afterwards. 'As a team result, we've done very well. We're ahead of Vettel. I'm sure they're [Ferrari] going to be tough [to beat], but we're ahead of who we need to be. We thought this was going to be a very tough one. It's turned out to be better than we ever expected.'

As for the race, though, Lando was again unable to capitalise as he was plagued by a hydraulic problem and was passed by Ricciardo on the final lap. However, the Aussie's move was clumsy and forced Norris off the track, which allowed both Kimi Räikkönen and Nico Hülkenberg through, and while Ricciardo was later hit with a five-second penalty and two penalty points on his super licence, it was no consolation for Norris who was placed down in ninth.

But his luck improved in Austria at the Red Bull Ring, a track where Norris was clearly comfortable. In qualifying, he finished sixth but was promoted to fifth on the grid due to a ten-place grid penalty for Kevin Magnussen. In the race, Norris battled Hamilton for third before eventually coming home in sixth place for another solid haul of points and a clean weekend.

Before the British Grand Prix at Silverstone, I was lucky to be invited to attend a media day that McLaren had organised at

Dunsfold Aerodrome, better known as the *Top Gear* test track. Norris and Sainz were set to provide rides for members of the media around the 2.82-kilometre circuit. Normally, the idea is for journalists to ask questions, but for the drivers, the day offered an opportunity to get some revenge on anybody who might have previously asked them difficult questions by tearing it around the track in McLaren 600LTs.

Thankfully, nobody succumbed to the powers of g-force, but throughout the day, it became apparent just how close Norris and Sainz had become. Sure, they were competitive, that much is expected for F1 teammates, but it was remarkable just how close their bond was. Norris still took on the role of the annoying little brother, but Sainz had clearly warmed to him.

After taking to the track, everyone drove to a local pub for some lunch. During the meal, we discussed Norris' new contract. After his comments in France, Norris had indeed managed to secure a new deal ahead of the British Grand Prix. It was an unprecedented move by McLaren, as he had only been an F1 driver for a handful of races, but his performances were attracting attention, and rather than risk losing him, they handed him a new improved contract.

The following day, details emerged of Norris' new contract, which was estimated to be worth around £2.5 million a year – some increase from his previous salary of £380,000. But what would he be buying to celebrate his new boost in earnings? 'I've not bought anything yet to celebrate the new contract,' he told me. 'I have started playing golf, but I need to get some skill before buying some new clubs.' And as for the negotiations? 'It was agreed just after Austria,' he explained, 'but I'd not spoken to the team much about it, I just got told by my manager that the team had extended it.'

As for McLaren's perspective, Brown said his team were always committed to signing Norris – and Sainz – for 2020 and wanted to ensure they got their business done before the driver transfer market, or 'silly season', kicked off. By tying up his driver pairing so early in the season, Brown had managed to fend off interest from any rival team and ensure the continuation of the team's success, which in turn would make life easier for the designers and engineers working on next season's car.

Brown said: 'With the driver market going on we wanted to be the first team to say what we're doing and next year was never in doubt. It was in our best interests that as silly season ramps up they go knocking on some other doors and McLaren have their head down. Lando is in a good place. We had a long-term relationship that has already been defined, so as he gets more successful and we get more successful, we all win together.'

The renewal came just ahead of the British Grand Prix in what is the team's home race, and Norris' first home race in F1. Would he be ready for the increased attention? 'A podium in F1 would be a lot cooler,' he admitted. 'The fans are great, seeing all their passion. When I started the season, I was really nervous before races but now it is much better. Having Carlos as my teammate makes it much better because we have fun together.'

As for the British GP itself, the Thursday pre-race conference offered the opportunity to speak to Norris about his coming of age in F1. It was apparent that his battle with Hamilton in the previous race in Austria had whetted his appetite and provided a glimpse of the changing of the guard when it comes to the future of British F1 talent. This had obviously caught the imagination of the media, but there was also a sense that Norris was starting to believe this narrative. After cutting his teeth in the opening few races, he was beginning to feel part of the F1 establishment. When asked about fighting for track position with Hamilton at the Red Bull Ring, Norris said: 'It would be disappointing if he retired before I had a chance to race him. He's British. He's the man. He's a five-time world champion. It's cool racing someone like that. With Lewis it's a combination of him being British and maybe the best driver ever. Those two things make racing him something I would love to do. It would be a shame if I don't get to do it.'

Unfortunately, Norris did not get a chance to go wheel-to-wheel with Hamilton at his first British Grand Prix as he finished out of the points in eleventh, while Hamilton won the race for a record sixth time.

In Germany, Norris was sent to the back of the grid at the Hockenheimring due to penalties accumulated for an unscheduled change of engine parts. His luck did not change during the weekend either as his team were caught out running on wet tyres for too long, while others pitted for the faster intermediate tyres. A power unit failure then caused him to retire from the race after only 25 laps.

Norris finished ninth in Hungary and eleventh in Belgium, despite a power failure on the final lap meaning he was unable to finish the race. However, the race at Spa was overshadowed by the tragic accident that killed F2 racer Anthoine Hubert on the day before the F1 Grand Prix race. Hubert was critically injured on the second lap of the feature race when he struck Ralph Boschung's car after Giuliano Alesi lost control as he went up the Raidillon curve, which caused Boschung to slow down. After hitting Boschung, Hubert was unable to prevent his own car from striking the barriers and the impact was so great that the Frenchman's car was spat out back into oncoming traffic, and he was struck by Juan Manuel Correa, who was unable to avoid the wreckage. Both cars were split apart and Hubert and Correa were rushed to hospital. Sadly, Hubert was pronounced dead approximately 90 minutes after the crash, while Correa required medical attention in Liège after breaking both his legs. The tragedy plunged motor sport into mourning, and before the Belgian GP race, a minute's silence was held and all cars carried a tribute to the racer, who was just 22.

Hubert's funeral took place on 10 September, two days after the Italian GP, and was attended by the FIA president, Jean Todt and a number of F1 drivers, including Charles Leclerc, Pierre Gasly and George Russell. For Norris, at the Italian GP in Monza, the race after the Belgian GP, he spoke about how the incident had impacted him and his family and raised questions as to whether he should continue to race, given the dangers.

Post-race, Norris admitted he was 'not feeling great' about racing, adding: 'What happened here on Saturday could happen to any of us. It could have been me last year racing in Formula Two. When you think like that, it starts shaking you. Maybe some people take it better than others, but I didn't take it too well.'

A few days later, ahead of the Italian GP, Norris was still reflecting on the tragedy and how it had affected him. 'The accident is still in my head and it will be, especially when I get back in the car,' he said. He also revealed that he had tried to reassure his family about his safety. He added: 'The crash threw my dad's mind because he comes to all the races. He sees it and knows a lot more. It hit my dad quite hard. He felt very sick. He had to go to the toilet to be sick.' While drivers take the danger in their stride, it is not so easy being the parent of an F1 racer: 'My dad is there with me all the time. He can't even watch my onboard camera for the start. He has to go somewhere and hide because he just doesn't want to see. So when it goes even worse, a situation like it was at Spa, he can't take it. It is the same for my mum. She is not there at the track that often, but she still worries, as she always does. I try and reassure them it will be OK because I think that's what you've got to say, but it almost makes it worse because I'm sure that's what every other driver said, and then we have what happened last weekend. It shows accidents can still happen. Everyone started to think it's not going to happen, everything is getting much better in terms of safety, but then it happens like that.'

Thankfully, the race at Monza passed without incident, but another grid penalty saw Norris start in sixteenth. He battled back to tenth and took a well-deserved point in what was the final race in the European leg of the season.

The Singapore GP always feels like the start to the season finale. After the long flight from Europe, racers are met with a different climate and what is one of the most spectacular races on the F1 calendar. The night race around the streets of Singapore is one of, if not the, toughest test on the schedule as the slightest mistakes are punishable by race-ending concrete walls; if a driver goes ever so slightly over the white line, they can lose a wing or a wheel and their race is over. However, Norris delivered a faultless drive to finish in seventh place, taking six points, while Sainz was down in twelfth and out of the points.

Another quirk with the Singapore GP is that despite the time difference, the racing schedule stays on European time. The race gets underway at 8pm, which means getting up around 2pm and going to bed around 5am – ideal for the post-race party. But not for Norris, who was spotted working in the paddock on the Sunday, helping strip down his car before it was flown off to Russia for the next leg. At the end of the night, he had to pretend to some fans that he was a McLaren mechanic as he made his way back to the hotel in grubby clothes with oily hands. His helping out in the garage emphasised how much he understood the long-term benefits of collaborating with the team around him, just as he had done in his karting days, and by staying on and lending a hand, he was earning their respect, which could be crucial when he needed them to go the extra mile for him, such as during a quick engine change in between qualifying sessions.

The following weekend, Norris was asked about his relationship with his mechanics. 'I get on well with my mechanics,' he said. 'I like to see them happy. They work harder on the car than I do, and it is nice to show you are on their side. Amber Lounge [the exclusive post-race nightclub that used to be the go-to place for the paddock to party after an F1 race at cities such as Monaco and Singapore] was all right but it is not something I get excited about. I was dreading it more and not wanting to go. It's not really me.'

Norris followed his Singapore performance with another solid return in Russia, finishing eighth in an otherwise dreary race in Sochi. However, the same cannot be said for the Japanese GP that followed two weeks later. Super Typhoon Hagibis was forecast to hit the Suzuka track on Saturday, bang on time for qualifying. Given the severity of the weather predicted, and the fact that a few years earlier, French driver Jules Bianchi had tragically lost his life as a result of injuries sustained following a crash in poor weather at Suzuka, it was unsurprising that there was concern in the paddock. Norris was just one of several F1 drivers who urged the sport's organisers – the FIA, F1 and the race promoter – to consider delaying qualifying for 24 hours while the storm passed. Thankfully, after a little persuading, all parties agreed, and instead, Max Verstappen organised a game of FIFA on the PlayStation, which Norris and Sainz agreed to take part in. Hunkered down in their hotel rooms, the wind and rain battered the area, with TV pictures showing widespread devastation, proving that it was definitely the right call to delay qualifying. The following day, on a busy and blustery day at Suzuka, Norris qualified in eighth place; however, in the race he was hit by Albon on the fourth lap, which caused damage to the McLaren's floor. He was then forced to make a pit stop when his brakes started to get too hot. The cause of the overheating was found to be some debris picked up from Leclerc's front wing, which had blocked the airflow into the brake duct. Consequently, Norris was unable to capitalise on his top-ten grid slot and finished out of the points in eleventh place.

There was more disappointment in Mexico as Norris was forced to withdraw from the race after 48 laps. A slow pit stop had resulted in his team sending him off without his front-left wheel being tightened and fitted correctly. Spotting the mistake, Norris pulled over at the top of the pit lane before entering the track, and his team had to push him back into the garage where they subsequently retired his car from the race.

The season continued the following weekend in Austin, which is arguably one of the most fun races on the calendar. The race in Texas has been incredibly popular ever since it was added to the schedule in 2012. Norris arrived in twelfth place in the standings; not bad for a rookie season in an uncompetitive car, particularly given the operational and mechanical failures he had endured. He impressed during the Saturday qualifying session, where he posted a time that would again see him start inside the top eight on the grid.

However, race day was mainly remembered for Ross Brawn's presentation on F1's vision of the future, which announced that the cars would soon be radically redesigned and also that there would be a budget cap introduced. The bigger teams had inflated their budgets to £400 million developing their cars over the course of the season, which made it incredibly difficult for the mid-table teams, such as McLaren, who were unable to challenge for wins. Brown hailed the rule changes as good news for the sport, saying: 'It's exciting, we're going to run at the budget cap. We are committed to getting back to winning world championships.'

In Sunday's race, Norris finished seventh, one place ahead of Sainz, while Hamilton's second place was enough to see him clinch his sixth world title.

The Brazilian Grand Prix has a history of serving up sensational racing and poignant moments. And the 2019 instalment was another fine example. As with many F1 races, it was the events in the stewards' room after the race that created the talking points. The podium ceremony took place with Verstappen having won the race and Hamilton and Gasly on the podium in second and third place respectively. Sainz had finished fourth and Norris in eighth. However, a five-second post-race penalty for Hamilton dropped him from second to seventh, meaning Sainz was later confirmed in P3. It was McLaren's first podium since the 2014 Australian GP. Sainz's promotion to the podium with Verstappen and Gasly meant the top three drivers were all graduates from Red Bull's Young Driver Programme. McLaren's staff recreated their own podium celebrations long after the fans had left the Interlagos circuit – and the partying continued long into the night.

Charlotte Sefton says that podium for Sainz became a defining moment for Norris – while he was taking part in the celebrations and the photographs, deep down, he wanted to be the one who had delivered that podium for the team. 'By the end of his first season,' she explains, 'Lando had started to show consistency but it was Carlos who definitely had the edge. That podium in Brazil when Lewis got his penalty was huge for us as a team. So many people in the team had never experienced a podium before. It was a bizarre weekend and Lando was in all the pictures. You could really tell that he was like, "I really want this. I really want to make the team happy."'

Norris closed out the season with an eighth-place finish in Abu Dhabi, having started the race in sixth, as he once again over-delivered on the Saturday and was then unable to convert that grid slot in the race. He ended the season in eleventh place in the drivers' championship standings – not bad considering he did not finish in six of the 21 races. Meanwhile, Sainz was sixth, behind the Ferrari duo of Leclerc and Vettel in what proved to be an impressive debut for his new team.

But there was something that Norris was struggling with during his first year in the sport – something that he did not open up about until two years later in a television interview. The public's perception of the nineteen-year-old who had become the UK's youngest F1 driver was that he did not take himself too seriously and enjoyed a practical joke. All of this was true, but as he explained to the presenters of *This Morning* on ITV in the UK in 2021, he had also been 'depressed a lot of the time' in his debut F1 season.

Of course, there will be those who point out that at nineteen years old and racing in F1, Norris was living out a life that many could only dream of and for that he should consider himself fortunate. But this kind of assessment completely fails to consider the pressure the young driver was putting himself under. He was delivering for McLaren, but was he doing enough? His whole life had been geared to reaching F1, and now he was there, he was working hard to ensure he stayed there and clearly any missed opportunity for points weighed heavily on him.

'I guess people, when you just watch TV, don't realise many things that a driver goes through,' he said in the interview. 'It's a bit of a shame, but there's more programmes now where you get to see what the driver is like behind the scenes, and the amount of pressure and stress that they have to cope with. Especially at my age, coming into Formula 1 at nineteen, there's a lot of eyes on you. So dealing with all these kinds of things, that took its toll on me. [I was] feeling like, I don't know what's next, if this goes wrong, if I don't go out in the next session and perform, what's the outcome of all of this? Am I going to be in F1 next year? If I'm not, what am I going to do? Because I'm not really good at many other things in life. So just all of that, and then feeling depressed a lot of time that if I have a bad weekend I just think, I'm not good enough and things like that. When they start adding up over a season, and the social media side of it all, that can just really start to hurt you.' He went on to reveal that he had only found the strength to speak out after getting a combination of support from the McLaren team and through working with the mental health charity Mind, which had led him to process and understand the worries and concerns that he had. 'I'm in a much better place now,' he concluded. 'I'm much happier and I can enjoy everything I do.'

PUT ON HOLD

The 2020 Australian Grand Prix was one of the strangest races I have attended for a number of reasons, but it also proved to be a seminal moment for F1. And what followed served to galvanise the teams and the commercial rights holders, Liberty Media. At the start of the year, as more cases of the Covid-19 virus were reported, there was a suspicion that preseason testing would be scrapped. It wasn't, and testing itself was unspectacular, although McLaren did compete a lot of laps – 802 times around the Circuit de Barcelona-Catalunya; only Ferrari and Mercedes did more, which pointed to an increase in reliability.

Mercedes also looked to have stolen the march on the rest of the paddock by developing their 'dual-axis steering' system, which meant their drivers could pull in the steering wheel to alter the toe of the front wheels. It was a brilliant concept and one the FIA were quick to rule out for the following year by making it illegal. But the real issue everyone was talking about was the spread of Covid-19 and the effect it might have on the F1 calendar.

As other sports began to adjust their schedules, F1 pressed ahead with plans for the season-opening race at Albert Park in Melbourne, scheduled for 15 March. There were concerns that the Italian-based teams – Ferrari and AlphaTauri – would not be granted entry to Australia as Italy was experiencing one of the worst outbreaks of the virus. As the clock counted down to the date of the first race, there was the feeling among the press that F1 would be forced to act and cancel in advance of thousands of new arrivals turning up at Melbourne airport. The threat of bringing the virus to Australia was highlighted by the local authorities, who called for the grand prix to be cancelled.

Arriving at Heathrow to get the flight to Hong Kong, which had reported its own mass outbreak, I was hesitant whether boarding the plane was the right thing to do. The majority of teams and members of the media who were due to fly via Hong Kong had rescheduled due to the increased risk not only of catching Covid-19 but in case the Australian government decided to change their immigration rules mid-flight, which would mean it would not be possible to disembark the plane after leaving Hong Kong.

During the stopover, I was shocked to see the airport so quiet. The terminal at Hong Kong is usually a bustling hub that connects Europe with Asia and Australia, filled with travellers sifting through the duty-free shops and eating in restaurants, but it was almost completely deserted, with just a handful of people shuffling around the place. However, landing in Australia, the overriding sense was that it was business as usual. The Thursday media was fairly routine, aside from some confusion about the implementation of Covid-19 protocols. There was no guidance from the FIA or F1 as to what was required, so many teams just made up their own rules. Drivers were urged not to shake hands with fans and to keep their distance, but otherwise there was little else in the way of instructions.

Russell and Norris were both asked, along with all the other drivers, if they felt it was right that F1 was pressing ahead with the race despite the unknown consequences of contracting Covid-19. Both gave similar answers that were heavily PR-influenced, saying they were happy to be in Australia for the start of the new season and had placed their faith in the FIA to make the right decision about whether it was right to have made the trip. Lewis Hamilton gave a slightly different response – when he was asked why F1 had allowed the teams to make the trip, he replied: 'Cash is king.' Three words that summed up how many in the paddock were feeling, but not willing to say so out loud. In some ways, Hamilton's remark started the ball rolling and from this point on the pressure mounted on F1 to call the event off.

That evening, McLaren reported that a team member had tested positive for Covid-19 and subsequently withdrew from the event. It was a bold move from the team, given they risked losing a haul of points, and this decision triggered some of the most interesting off-track moments in F1 history. The conversations and lobbying went on through the night as F1's CEO Chase Carey flew in from Vietnam, where he was seeking reassurances from the race organisers that the new track would be ready in time for the inaugural Vietnam Grand Prix later in the season. It transpired that there were two camps: those teams who wanted to go ahead and race, and those who supported McLaren's decision to withdraw and wanted to follow suit.

Come Friday morning, it was still not clear which way the decision would go. Local radio had members of the Australian Grand Prix telling fans to head to the track as the race was still going ahead, but members of the media were told that it was still hanging in the balance. As the queues formed at the gates in preparation for Friday's practice sessions, the decision was made to postpone the race. There followed a mad scramble to return to Europe, with the majority of teams rebooking flights to leave on Saturday.

Soon after the postponement, a number of races were either cancelled altogether or suspended as the season was placed on hold. But while the racing stopped, drivers found other ways to keep busy. Norris used his social media channels to engage with fans and raise money for charity. By the end of March, he had taken part in a Twitch Stream Aid event alongside a number of musicians and celebrities, which raised more than $2.2 million for the Covid-19 Solidarity Response Fund. Norris had promised to shave his head if he passed the $10,000 total he had personally set. An anonymous donation of $700 took him over the goal, sending him into a fit of laughter, adding: 'No! We made 10k! RIP hair!' After buying some hair clippers on Amazon, he later added on Instagram: 'Thanks to all my viewers for raising over $12,000 by the end total for Twitch Stream Aid and the fight against Covid-19. I do have to cut all my hair off now though.' Sainz was quick to reply to the post and added: 'Oh boy I'm ready.'

The break in racing was filled with that of a virtual kind, which was right up Norris' street given his love of gaming and the fact that F1 drivers can regularly spend around seven hours a day in the team's simulator as they try to refine their car's set-up in advance of a race. When the Chinese Grand Prix was postponed, F1 launched the Esports Virtual Grand Prix series, starting with the Bahrain GP, which was the second race on the original calendar. A press release from F1 confirmed the plan: 'The series has been created to enable fans to continue watching F1 races virtually, despite the ongoing Covid-19 situation that has affected this season's opening race calendar. The virtual races will run in place of every postponed Grand Prix, starting this weekend with the Virtual Bahrain Grand Prix on Sunday 22 March. Every subsequent race weekend will see the postponed real-world F1 race replaced with a Virtual Grand Prix, with the initiative currently scheduled to run until May. The first race of the series will see current F1 drivers line up on the grid alongside a host of stars to be announced in due course.' The 28-lap race proved to be good fun, but of course it was no replacement for the real thing.

That said, there was plenty of needle when Norris fell out with Indy 500 champion, Simon Pagenaud. Norris was competing in a virtual IndyCar race and leading the field when he was deliberately wiped out by Pagenaud, who won the IndyCar series in 2016 and the 2019 Indy 500 race. Somewhat pathetically, Pagenaud protested his innocence but was caught out by footage on his live stream recording him saying, 'we take Lando out, let's do it', before he slowed down and forced Norris into the back of him. Pagenaud tried to play innocent by saying he lost control, but once footage was aired from his webcam, fans were sent into meltdown. Norris, who had already won one virtual IndyCar race, said: 'He apologised? He said he wanted to come into the pits and he wanted to slow me up, and he didn't want me to win. Do you know how many hours, how much time I put into the left [turn]? How many hours I've spent driving in a straight line and then just doing this. I must have spent a day in total, I reckon I've spent 24 hours driving in a straight line and turning left, trying to perfect it. With the most delicate touch, I've tried doing it one-handed, with my knee … 24 hours! And then because that guy gets a bit salty that a non-IndyCar driver is about to win an Indy race, it just ruins it. So, yeah, that's that.' Norris eventually saw the funny side, especially when he relayed the story to Verstappen, who is also a keen gamer. The Dutchman watched the incident back and said to Norris on a live stream, 'This is really the stupidest thing I've ever seen. How stupid to say live that you are going to crash someone. If you're planning something like that, you don't say it live!'

Aside from the virtual racing, the UK-based teams also put in an incredible effort to help local hospitals by producing ventilators after the government announced that there was a shortage of the equipment used to treat the most seriously ill patients. But the reality was that as the months ticked past with no races, many teams were left struggling financially. There was never any official announcement from McLaren, but well-placed sources said that both Norris and Sainz agreed to take pay cuts to help McLaren save jobs. The team had already furloughed some staff – putting them on a temporary leave of absence on a reduced salary supported by the government. Brown was acutely aware how it was affecting his team and stated that some teams would be facing bankruptcy unless racing resumed: 'Could I see – through what is going on right now in the world – if we don't tackle this situation head on very aggressively – two teams disappearing? Yeah. In fact, I could see four teams disappearing if this isn't handled the right way. I don't think the timing could be worse from that standpoint. F1 is in a very fragile state at the moment.'

Despite there being no racing, the F1 news was relentless. One big story that broke in May was the news that Daniel Ricciardo would be joining McLaren for 2021. The details were clear. Norris already had his long-term deal, and the Aussie would be arriving to partner him in the team. In doing so, it freed up Sainz to join Ferrari, after he had been heavily linked with the Italian team. The development meant that the bromance between Norris and Sainz would be broken up at the end of the 2020 season, but McLaren would be recruiting a popular figure in Sainz's place – and more importantly a race-winner. Ricciardo would arrive from Renault, just as Sainz had done before him, where the Australian had endured a frustrating few seasons since leaving Red Bull.

For Brown, it was a no-brainer, Sainz wanted to go to Ferrari, and he had finally signed Ricciardo at the second attempt, having missed out when he initially went to Renault. 'Signing Daniel is another step forward in our long-term plan and will bring an exciting new dimension to the team, alongside Lando,' said

Brown. 'This is good news for our team, partners and of course our fans. I also want to pay tribute to Carlos for the excellent job he has been doing for McLaren in helping our performance-recovery plan. He is a real team player and we wish him well for his future beyond McLaren.'

Among the media, there was a feeling that both Ricciardo and Norris had similar personalities, which would certainly liven things up for the team in the form of practical jokes, but there was already a question mark as to what the change would do for Norris' development. McLaren were keen to lean on the Aussie's experience. Despite an impressive debut season, the expectation was such that Ricciardo would become McLaren's de-facto No. 1 driver. In the accompanying press release, the McLaren team principal, Andreas Seidl, almost hinted as much, saying: 'Daniel is a proven race-winner and his experience, commitment and energy will be a valuable addition to McLaren and our mission to return to the front of the field. With Daniel and Lando as teammates, I believe we have two racers who will continue to excite our fans and help the team grow.'

Approaching midway through the year, it became clear that F1 was going to try and bring the sport back, despite the pandemic. Some domestic football leagues had already restarted, even though there were some concerns among players about the risks involved. There had been plenty of meetings with the UK government over a race at Silverstone, and F1 were in discussion with other promoters and circuits for updates on local Covid-19 policies. It is all very well bringing back a domestic football championship involving no fans, but trying to organise races for the global sporting event that is Formula One in the middle of a pandemic created a logistical nightmare, and F1 does not get the credit it deserves for pulling it off.

Each country and city had their own protocols, and with participants arriving from across the world, it all became a rather complicated puzzle. Flights continued to operate, albeit on reduced schedules, and hotels were desperate for business. But the biggest task was aligning all the paperwork required to travel. Taking Covid-19 tests and getting the results back within an allotted time scale required precision and planning, as did the testing process and policies at each individual track. However, by now it was absolutely clear that the drivers and their teams would be prepared to do anything to go racing again.

I caught up with Norris on a video call where he said he and his fellow drivers in the Grand Prix Drivers' Association were all fully behind the restart at the Red Bull Ring in Austria. Unlike in football, there seemed to be no reservations about catching the virus. It was very clear as to what was required and that teams would be operating within their bubbles, with no mixing with other outfits. Press and media were kept away in a separate part of the track and there were of course no fans. Norris had been briefed by his trainer as to what the requirements were, with warnings in place for breaches.

'All the drivers have someone they are speaking to in terms of their own safety. I have my trainer who has done all his research and will look after me. But everyone has their own ideas and ways to stay at their best, but we are all hungry to get back doing what we love doing. So long as we all stick to the guidelines and what we should do, then everyone is happy to go back to racing cars,' Norris said.

One aspect he was less enamoured with was the Covid-19 tests he was required to do, almost on a daily basis: 'I have had quite a few tests. You have to stick an earbud that is like three times as long and put it in your nose. Every time you do it, it is a bit weird and you want to throw up. It doesn't hurt. It is not as bad as getting a needle in your arm. You just see this large cotton bud in front of your face and you see it disappear and you are like "ugh" and it's at the back of your head.'

I was also able to ask Norris about Sainz's move to Ferrari, which had since been confirmed by the Italian team. The two had obviously become close, and while he was sad to see him go, he was more jealous about the fact Sainz would now be in position to fight for wins in a more competitive car. 'Ferrari is one of the top three teams at the moment,' he said, 'so anyone who gets the chance to go there has done a fricking good job to achieve that. That's what Carlos did and I am happy for him, but I am also happy with where I am and I believe we can improve as a team. With Daniel coming on board, a guy known for winning races, I am happy that we can take that next step as a team. But that said, everyone is jealous and now Carlos is going to be in with a chance of winning races and that has always been my dream.'

In the meantime, though, Lando was just eager to get back to racing in F1 and had spent a day or two driving his old Formula 3 car to get his eye in as McLaren were unable to borrow engines from old supplier Honda to run their own F1 cars. Honda would have retained the power units from the previous season, plus the FIA have strict rules about what older models can be used, while Pirelli would also have been required to provide suitable tyres. Ultimately, it proved easier to switch back to using the F3 car. 'It was good to be back in the mentality of driving a car and being on the limit,' Lando said about the testing session, 'of course it would feel better driving an F1 car but we won't be blaming the result in Austria on the fact we have not driven one as a test. It just might take us a little longer to get back into it, but we should be up to speed pretty quickly.'

Lando definitely did not expect to kick off the delayed 2020 season with a podium – his first in F1 – at the opening round in Austria. It came after Hamilton was hit with a five-second penalty for causing a collision with Albon. That dropped the Mercedes man, who had finished second, out of the top three, promoting Norris, who had finished fourth. In doing so, he became the third-youngest podium finisher in Formula One history at twenty years and 235 days old. Even though the podium came as a result of Hamilton's penalty, it was certainly no fluke. Norris had been made aware that the world champion would be getting the time added on, so he hammered out a final lap that was the quickest of the race to ensure he benefited. The hardest part was trying to breathe afterwards with a facemask saturated in champagne from the podium celebration. Panting his way through the post-race press conference, he asked for a new facemask, adding: 'I am speechless. There were a few points in the race where I thought I had fudged it up. But I did not give up. I kept on going and I ended up on the podium. When Lewis' penalty came up, I had to turn it up and go fishing and I managed to get him on the final lap. No matter what record you break – unless it's the youngest winner ever – I am just happy to be on the podium. It is a nice bonus to have but I am here to win races and do well. I'm so happy and so proud of the team, considering where we were a couple of years ago. I'm proud to be part of it.'

The strict Covid-19 protocols did mean that the celebrations were largely muted, with the team unsure what they were allowed to do.

'It was all really weird because he just got the trophy presented to him on a platform on a plinth,' said Sefton. 'Only a few people were allowed up to see it because you weren't allowed to move out of your garage space. So Mark and John were there and so too was Zak. He gave Lando a massive hug and crushed his ribs; he was complaining about it for days afterwards. We were all so pleased for Lando, but we also wanted to have a straightforward podium where we could all go up the pit lane and celebrate it and spray champagne. We missed that but because of the rules it was all over the shop and we had no plans on how to celebrate.'

Another person who was particularly happy to see Norris take his first F1 podium was Trevor Carlin. He had nurtured Norris' career and finally was seeing him come good at the top level of motor sport. The fact that he was able to pip Hamilton to the podium proved in Carlin's mind that Norris would be the racer to carry the mantle once Hamilton retired.

'Lando is the obvious heir to Lewis' crown as the top British driver,' he said, obviously rating Norris above Russell. 'When Lewis achieves everything he needs to achieve and steps down, Lando will be at the helm. He needs the correct package, but McLaren have made incredible steps over the past few months and who's to say that they cannot be a force in twelve months' time? He is doing everything right and the results are coming and I am very proud of him.'

It was refreshing to speak to Carlin about his time mentoring Norris, and as well as Hamilton, he drew on a comparison with Vettel, who had also raced for him in the junior categories. 'Will Lando change from a lifestyle point of view? Absolutely not,' he said. 'He is not that sort of guy. A great example is Sebastian Vettel because he was racing with us in 2006 and 2007. I saw him at Hockenheim two years ago when his younger brother was doing an Audi support race and Seb was doing his brother's pit board. I went over and asked him how he was doing and I said: "Hey, Seb, mind if I tell you something? … You have never changed." Now, it has been years since he drove for me and [he] is a four-time world champion and has all the money in the world. He just looked at me and replied: "Why would I need to?" and I see Lando being exactly the same. Lando is the nicest person you could ever meet. I am chuffed to bits for him. He is not flash or big-headed. He basically always delivers. It is as simple as that.'

Podium aside, perhaps the biggest change that was evident from Norris' experiences in F1 was his recognition that the sport was giving him a platform for good. For the majority of young drivers, they are only focused on achieving their goal of reaching F1. If they get there, there is a slight hesitancy to speak about anything other than racing; lap times, car set-up, track conditions. This is understandable, it is the subject they know best, and they have usually been thoroughly briefed by their communications teams not to say anything that could get them into trouble.

However, this also means that some drivers can come across as being rather boring. People often speak about the great personalities of motor sport's past – drivers such as James Hunt or Sir Stirling Moss. We are missing the big characters in this modern era of F1, but the reality is those characters are there, they just have not been allowed to express themselves in the way that drivers did in the past. It is no coincidence that McLaren's decision to run frequent media sessions with Norris and the key journalists within the paddock has seen him become more confident with dealing with the media. Watching him go from nervous teen to confident F1 driver has been an incredible transformation, and one which the sport needed.

During Norris' time, Hamilton and Vettel have taken the lead in terms of addressing the wider issues surrounding F1. Both drivers have spoken out about climate change and racism, plus other social issues, while other drivers on the grid have been largely quiet on such subjects. Ahead of the British Grand Prix at Silverstone, racism was once again at the top of the news agenda, following the murder of George Floyd in Minneapolis, which led to the Black Lives Matter protest movement spreading around the world. At the previous Austrian, Styrian and Hungarian Grand Prix, the execution of the anti-racist 'We

Race As One' initiative was shambolic. Some drivers wore 'End Racism' T-shirts, while others did not wear them. Some did not even line up alongside their fellow stars. It prompted much criticism and forced F1 to intervene and create a more coherent approach. The drivers were split as to whether they would take a knee or not, many had raised their concerns privately, and some had publicly spoken about whether they would make the gesture, which was being done in other sports, mainly football. It was ultimately decided that drivers could chose to take the knee if they wanted, but the half-measures made it look like the grid was split, rather than aligned on the anti-racism message. Hamilton was vocal about the issue, accusing F1 and the FIA of 'lacking leadership'. So, when Norris was asked about the important anti-racism message that F1 was running with an 'End Racism' protest planned before the British Grand Prix, it was refreshing to see that instead of skirting the issue, he addressed it head-on.

'We are united in agreeing with what we support as a community of F1 drivers,' he said with a new-found maturity. 'Whether we do take the knee or we don't take the knee, that is not the question. I don't think that needs to be the reason why people judge some of us to be in support of it or not. We all support it, no matter what. Over the past few weekends, the only one that was prepared for was round one, when there was an "End Racism" carpet down and we had to be there one minute prior to normal. Nothing was planned for the second or third race and no one spoke up in the briefing about what we were going to do. We are all in agreement that we want to do something. Some people want to do different things, but we are all in agreement that we want to take a stand and show something in support of what we're trying to do against racism. We will have a better structure and better plan in place for this weekend. Yes, it was a bit of a mess in Hungary. We have to accept that. But it wasn't the drivers' fault entirely. Whether we take a knee or not, we all want to have the same impact to support the situation we are in and are up against. I take a knee because that is most meaningful for the situation we are in. I want to have the biggest impact I can on ending racism. It is one of the few times in life when people like me or us as drivers can have an impact on the future, what we're going through just now and all the talk of equality and racism. This is one of the biggest initiatives around the world to go up against something and make a change going into the future and shape it in some way. I want to do everything I can.'

The 2020 British Grand Prix was held on 2 August, and a special one-off 70th Anniversary Grand Prix was organised for the following week. Both events were held at Silverstone, but Covid-19 protocols meant that no fans were allowed to attend. The drivers had by now become used to the lack of fans at races, just as they had become used to the daily Covid-19 tests, but this did not make it any more enjoyable.

'We call it the home race because of the fans,' said Norris ahead of Silverstone. 'When they are not there it's very difficult to call it a home race. You're just racing on your home track without it having any proper meaning or atmosphere. Why it was so cool last year was because of all the fans. That's what makes it special. It's not just the fact it's the country I was born in. The reason everyone loves their home race is because of the fans. When you don't have the fans, it doesn't mean as much, it's not as cool, it's not as special.'

That said, Norris did make one fan happy – six-year-old Eva Muttram, who designed his helmet for the race as part of a competition he ran on social media. Muttram had drawn the graphic by hand and it had then been transferred onto Lando's helmet for the race – complete with two love hearts. 'It reminds me a lot of when I was younger,' said Norris when talking about the helmet on social media, referring to his own passion for design, 'drawing away, just when I was like five, six, seven years old, printing off hundreds of helmet designs, colouring them in and doing whatever. It's very different from what I'm used to. All this glitz and glamour and sparkly bits and swooshes and cool stuff, I just went with something that reminded me of me when I was young. I love it. It's a lot of white, but at the same time, I just think it's really cute. I like the colours, and it's very original.'

Norris' reputation in F1 and among the younger fans on social media was flourishing. He was coming into his home race in fourth place in the drivers' championship. And F1's ability to get racing during the pandemic, albeit behind closed doors, was offering the public some much-needed entertainment. As a result, the twenty-year-old's profile was beginning to increase among the wider public. Andy Dunn, writing for the *Daily Mirror*, said in an article that Norris had 'been one of the eyecatchers' of the season, before adding that 'while his progress from success in the junior ranks to the top level has been eagerly monitored by motor-sport aficionados, he remains a relative unknown to the country's wider public. That could change over the next couple of weekends at Silverstone if the McLaren driver can continue the aggressive form that saw him finish third and fifth in the first two races of the season.'

Norris was feeling confident too. He had made a good start to the season and had a podium, and while he was getting to grips with his McLaren, the likes of Ferrari were struggling. He was also looking forward to putting on a show for the British public watching from home.

'It's a good opportunity to put myself out to the British fans, the British people, absolutely,' he said ahead of the race. 'It does not change the way I go about things but it is a chance for me, if I do well, to get myself out there. Because of the situation we are in, more people might tune in to watch Formula One this weekend. Also, at no point last season did we ever consider trying to beat them (Ferrari) – they were always out of our league. They have taken a big step backwards, in terms of lap time anyway, and we've taken a small step forward. Red Bull still have a very good package when they nail everything – better car than ours 100 per cent – but for whatever reason, they seem to have a more complicated car. We are at least in a position where we can capitalise on our opportunities on a much more regular basis. If we want to compete for championships, we are a long, long way behind Mercedes. But we are more competitive, so that is a good thing.'

Norris arrived at Silverstone on 30 June, having returned from spending some time at home with his mum and dad. In doing so, they'd all tested regularly for Covid-19 given the strict rules F1 had put in place. Senior figures at Silverstone had been working alongside the government to ensure that the race was able to go ahead. Despite there being no fans present, there were still close to 5,000 people attending, which included drivers, members of the media, mechanics, engineers, catering teams, cleaners and marshals. The announcement that the races would take place had been made in April by Silverstone's managing director Stuart Pringle, who had underlined the strict conditions that they would be operating under. A few months before the race, he had promised ticket holders that their purchases would be rolled over to 2021. From a driver's perspective, the situation was clear: should a driver arrive at Silverstone for the pre-race Covid-19 test and the result come back positive, then they would be required, in accordance with the UK's policy at the time, to self-isolate for ten days. Any driver testing positive, given that the British Grand Prix was quickly followed by the second anniversary race at Silverstone, taking place the week after, would likely be ruled out of both races and the potential for some decent championship points. And this is indeed what happened to Sergio Pérez, who missed both legs because he tested positive after taking a private plane to visit his mother in Mexico after she had been in hospital.

Norris was very conscious of the implications of testing positive and stuck to the guidelines. 'Of course it [a positive test] crosses our minds,' he said when he was asked about his precautions before his home race, 'if, for whatever reason you got it, you would at least be out for one race, possibly two, depending on when you got it. We will take as many precautions as we can. I went home to see my parents, but they got tested, everyone I saw got tested before I went down to make sure and then I came back, and I've not seen anyone since. It does go through our minds but as long as we do what we need to and we take the precautions we need to, then everything should be fine.' His prudence paid off too, for he finished fifth in the race, remaining in fourth place in the championship – ahead of Ferrari drivers Leclerc and Vettel.

Ahead of the second race at Silverstone, an interview appeared in *The Sunday Times* that served to introduce the young driver to the paper's readers. Norris' reputation in F1 was growing, but in the piece he is described as being the son of 'a multimillionaire businessman who has appeared in *The Sunday Times* Rich List'. The article goes on to explain how 'Norris attended the fee-paying Millfield School in Somerset, but left before his GCSEs to focus on his driving career'. However, it is Norris' characteristically honest quotes about his daily routine that feature in the piece that are the most revealing. 'My flat [in Woking] is near the McLaren headquarters,' he explained, 'but most of the time I stay in a hotel wherever I'm racing. I get up at 8am, although sometimes there's a knock at the door because I forget to set the alarm. I'm a "twentyteen", so I like to leave it as late as possible. Then I shower and listen to music. I like chilled stuff, I don't need anything heavy to psych me up for a day on the track. Breakfast is scrambled or poached eggs on brown toast. Occasionally, I sneak in a *pain aux raisins*, but my trainer doesn't approve. My trainer drives me to the track, which means I can sit in the back and watch something like *Money Heist* on Netflix. I hate driving myself because you never know what other drivers are going to do. It's far more dangerous on the road than a race circuit.'

The author, Jeremy Taylor, asked Norris about his podium in Austria and, again, Norris' honest response is what is most striking. 'I poured a bottle of champagne over my head on the podium,' Norris explained, 'because I didn't want to drink it. I find alcohol pretty disgusting, which is unusual for a twenty-year-old. I don't drink or smoke and prefer to be at home alone than partying in London. I spend downtime racing against my friends on a computer. That's how I relax when I'm not driving a 230-mph car. I don't have space for a girlfriend, either. It's not something I'm fussed about. If you want to be the best, you have to make sacrifices.'

In the build-up to the race, the media focus centred on Lewis Hamilton, who had won three races in a row and was again looking odds-on favourite to win the F1 title. Unsurprisingly, Norris was asked about his countryman's achievements, and he was full of praise for what Hamilton had done. Acknowledging that they were still operating in very different leagues, Norris hailed Hamilton's record-breaking achievements, but he also added that Hamilton would not have been able to achieve the same success had he been driving a McLaren rather than a Mercedes.

'They [Hamilton and his teammates] have been driving for the past few years with a massive advantage over every other team. Mercedes have been the best with the car, the best with the engine and that has allowed him to achieve the things he has. If Lewis was in a McLaren, he wouldn't look as good as what he has done. Mercedes have been so dominant, it's not been often they have had to race many other cars. But I don't think you can take anything away from him. He's had some good teammates in Rosberg and Bottas. Especially with Bottas, he has clearly had the upper hand on him the whole time they have been at Mercedes,' he said in his pre-race press conference.

'The records are something that will probably not be beaten,' he continued. 'He joined in a race-winning car and we are very far from that. He joined F1 when you could do as many test days as you wanted so he came in with a lot more experience than new drivers do nowadays. And he's pretty much always been in a race-winning car.' All of which was true, even if it did run against the positive narrative of Hamilton surging towards another world title.

Norris was ninth in F1's 70th anniversary race at Silverstone, and in the following race in Barcelona he finished tenth as McLaren's rivals – most notably Racing Point – started to make some improvements, even though there were some questions raised about the legality of their car. The team's challenger looked to have borrowed much of the design from the Mercedes from the previous season, and it was dubbed the 'pink Mercedes'.

Norris was seventh in Belgium, having qualified in tenth, in an otherwise dreary race that was dominated by Hamilton, who led for every lap. In the lead up to the race, Norris decided to ditch a helmet design that reflected his family's Belgian heritage. He had considered using the Flemish flag as a nod to his grandparents; however, McLaren stopped the design after discovering the image of a black lion on a yellow background was being used by a nationalist movement in Flanders. Consequently, there was a fear that such a helmet design could be viewed as a political statement, which is against the sport's rules.

If the Belgian Grand Prix was a procession, the 2020 Italian Grand Prix was anything but – a race that had everything, apart from the fans, who were still being kept away from racetracks as part of the Covid-19 protocols, although that would soon change after the race in Monza. Unlike some of the venues on the F1 calendar, the Italian GP always has the potential to provide a thrilling race owing to the high-speed nature of the track. It is interesting to think that despite some modern circuits being constructed from scratch, they still often serve up dull races with little overtaking, while classic old tracks such as Monza, Suzuka and Interlagos constantly deliver excitement. The 2020 instalment of the Italian GP served up a surprise winner in Pierre Gasly, while Sainz was second and Stroll third, making it one of the most unique podiums in years, as there were no Red Bull, Mercedes or Ferrari cars inside the top four. Norris came home in fourth place, narrowly missing out on his second podium by less than three seconds. His fourth-place finish, and Stroll's third place, meant the two were tied in the drivers' championship on 57 points behind Hamilton, Bottas and Verstappen.

Norris was having such a good season that he had started joking with Sainz that the Spaniard might have been better off staying with McLaren for 2021. Vettel and Leclerc had been hampered by reliability issues at Ferrari, and the Italian team were quickly sinking down the title championship, which was especially awkward given that the upcoming 2020 Tuscan Grand Prix was supposed to celebrate the team's 1,000th race in Formula One. There was even a special deep red team livery designed to mark the occasion with the drivers wearing special overalls and helmet designs. The team hosted a special event ahead of the F1 race, which was held at the Mugello Circuit. It was also the first time that spectators were allowed to attend races in 2020, following the previous eight races taking place behind closed doors. At Mugello, 2,880 spectators were granted tickets, and it was great to see the sensible measures that were being taken to help prevent the spread of the virus. That said, a fair few more fans pitched up outside the circuit walls to catch a glimpse of some sections of the track. Nonetheless, there was a real sense of achievement on the part of F1, the FIA, the teams and the media given that many sporting events were still taking place without any fans. Finally, after months of lockdowns and rigorous Covid-19 tests, fans were being allowed back into the circuits – and with this came a sense that the world was also beginning to return to normality.

The race in Tuscany was set in a beautiful location and there was a good mood in the paddock ahead of the race, partly brought about by the podium result at the previous race. Norris was feeling positive and revealed that, given Ferrari's capitulation, he had been enjoying winding up Sainz by saying that he would be passing him on track next season as McLaren hoped to beat them in the constructors' championship battle. 'There have been a few jokes. I'm not going to lie,' said Norris, 'but nothing which is rubbing it in. I know how karma works and how easily things can go the opposite way. We're going to go to some races where Ferrari will beat McLaren quite easily and Carlos will be the one saying, "Look who's laughing now." But we have an opportunity to fight them throughout the season. Ferrari seem to be in a difficult position at the moment with what they are trying to do and achieve. It would mean a lot to us as a team to take the next step and beat a team that's been front-running for many years to show the progress we have made.' Norris' words came back to bite him during practice as he crashed out, but he was still adamant he was right to stay put at McLaren, adding: 'Growing up I loved cars and supported McLaren more than any other team. Ferrari are one of the coolest teams, but I am happier to be in a McLaren.' The race itself was chaotic and saw Norris come from eleventh on the grid to finish sixth, while

Sainz was involved in a collision after only five laps and was forced to retire.

Sainz was the victim of another crash at the Russian GP, while Norris also finished outside of the points. By this point it was clear that the two were incredibly close, and golf had become a big part of their friendship. There was the banter but there was also a competitiveness between the two, which was driving McLaren forward as a team in what had become a dream partnership for Brown to manage. Due to the stringent Covid-19 protocols, it was not possible to see just how much time the pair spent together, for they were rarely seen together, but that does not mean to say they did not still hang out.

'They got on really well,' recalls Charlotte Sefton. 'We were at the Eifel Grand Prix at the Nürburgring and it was really cold and wet. We did not have our usual Brand Centre motorhome and instead had some temporary building in the paddock. The marketing office we worked in was tiny and was next to the drivers' room. The walls were paper-thin, so you could hear everything. We still had strict rules in place with people put into bubbles and then they could work in their subgroups. During Covid-19 and because of what happened in Australia, my job was literally all about keeping Lando and Carlos away from people. I felt like a zookeeper at times!'

Sefton and McLaren's caution was justified as during the Eifel GP that October, Stroll withdrew from the race complaining of feeling sick, and it later turned out that he had Covid-19. But as Sefton says, keeping their drivers apart proved extremely difficult. 'During the race weekend at the Nürburgring, it felt like there was a load of time just hanging around all weekend because the sessions were delayed. We were working in the marketing office and we could hear this giggling from the drivers' room next door … I went into their drivers' room to speak to them and they were both lying on the massage bed watching YouTube or Instagram videos together. We all started pissing ourselves laughing at first, but I then said to them, "What the fuck are you doing? Why aren't you in the garage? Everyone is looking for you!" I was like an ogre telling them off all the time. But that was the point where I and some others in the team realised that they actually enjoyed spending time together.'

The race itself offered Norris a potential haul of points as, despite the conditions, he looked fairly comfortable and qualified in eighth place, ahead of Sainz and Vettel's Ferrari. During the race, Norris had made it up to sixth place before he complained over the radio of a power issue. There was a chance that the electrical fault could be resolved on the pit wall through a series of remote procedures. However, on lap 44, the power issue proved to be terminal and his car suffered a total engine failure, which caused him to grind to a halt at the edge of the track at Turn Six.

It was not to be the end of Norris' frustrations either, as he went on to suffer a hat-trick of races with no points. His DNF in Germany was annoying, but it was nothing compared to frustration he would feel at the Portuguese Grand Prix.

The weekend had started well, and once again Norris had looked strong in practice and was third-quickest in FP2. However, the practice session will mainly be remembered for a collision between Stroll and Verstappen, which led to the Dutchman calling the Racing Point driver a 'mongol' over the team's radio, a comment that would later be widely condemned, including by the Mongolian government.

Stroll also caused issues for Norris later in the weekend as the Canadian made a complete mess of his overtake on lap eighteen in the feature race. He ran out of talent at Turn One and made contact with Norris. 'What the fuck is this dickhead doing?' asked Norris in an uncharacteristic outburst over his team's radio that was subsequently played out on air, albeit with the swearing cut out. Stroll was punished by the stewards for causing the clash with a five-second penalty, which was of no use to the Brit, whose damaged McLaren limped home in thirteenth place.

While Norris was still smarting, Hamilton took the chequered flag for the 92nd win of his F1 career. It was a landmark that moved him clear of the record held by Michael Schumacher. But Norris, who was still in a funk, gave a flippant response to a media question about his fellow Brit's achievement, which ultimately came back to bite him. 'I'm just happy for Lewis, nothing more,' he was quoted by the RaceFans website. 'It doesn't mean anything to me really. He's in a car which should win every race, basically. He has to beat one or two other drivers, that's it. Fair play to him, he's still doing the job he has to do.'

The quotes spread quickly across social media and, sensing the swell of criticism, and perhaps after being shown the error of his judgement by his management team, Norris took to social media to apologise for his remarks about Hamilton and his swearing at Stroll. He wrote on Twitter: 'I owe an apology. I've been stupid and careless with some things I've said lately in media and interviews, and I haven't shown the respect I should have to certain people. I'm not that kind of person, so I know I should apologise to them but also everyone reading/listening. Sorry.' But he was still smarting about the incident with Stroll, however, saying after the race how he was perplexed by the Canadian driver's actions. 'I don't know what he was doing, really,' he said to the media. 'He went to the left, I didn't know where he was. He went to the left which I was quite surprised by when he could very easily have gone for the inside. And I was easily halfway alongside, he just turned in.'

By the next race, the Emilia-Romagna Grand Prix at Imola, Norris' comments about Hamilton were still a talking point among the media. Some websites started digging into the relationship between the two drivers and old quotes resurfaced in which Norris described how Hamilton had had little influence on his own career. It was a perfect reminder of how comments could be taken out of context and how they could be manipulated to paint a specific picture. Norris had publicly apologised, and when he caught up with the British media in Imola, he said that he had also reached out to Hamilton privately to say sorry for any offence he might have caused. 'I sent Lewis a message to apologise,' he said. 'I don't know if he knew about it at the time, but I never meant to say something like that in a bad way or put any bad light on him at all. I respect everything he's done to achieve what he's done. It's incredible no matter what. It's just the way I put it was not the way I wanted it to come across. I apologised and I've just got to move on.' Hamilton did not shed any light on the conversation they had, which is not surprising given how he is well aware of how stories can spring up out of nowhere.

At the following race in Turkey, Hamilton wrapped up a record-equalling seventh world title in Istanbul in tricky conditions. It was an impressive drive from the Brit, who won the race from sixth place on the grid. His title-winning drive was hailed as one of the best performances in his career as he plotted his way around Istanbul Park with precision. Hamilton was hailed by many senior F1 figures as he equalled Schumacher's total of titles, and there was also a call for him to be knighted by the Queen in recognition of his success. Norris, who himself had had a good race, going from fourteenth on the grid – largely due to a penalty for failing to slow for yellow flags – came across the line in eighth. He also picked up a bonus point for setting the fastest lap. Post-race, learning from his mistake a few weeks earlier, Norris was quick to praise Hamilton. 'Only one person in the world has achieved what he has,' he said, 'and that's Michael Schumacher, so he has led the way in many aspects, on the track but also off the track. A lot of athletes who have done such things in other sports have got knighthoods so I see no reason why he shouldn't. It is a good thing for kids who want to get into racing, or who don't know much about racing, to be inspired by him and obviously try and achieve similar things to what he's done.'

The 2020 Bahrain Grand Prix will forever be remembered as the location of one of the most miraculous escapes in F1 history, up there with Lauda being pulled from the wreckage of his burning Ferrari at the Nürburgring. On the first lap, Romain Grosjean clipped the AlphaTauri of Daniil Kvyat and ricocheted into the barrier on the straight after Turn Three. 'Unbelievably, Grosjean managed to escape from his Haas after it had literally been split in two and burst into flames and was wedged in the metal barrier. Having since watched the footage back, it is difficult to understand how the Frenchman escaped with his life. There was no doubt that he was saved by the halo cockpit protection system, while the four layers of fire-protective clothing bought him crucial seconds of protection from the flames, while British doctor Ian Roberts and South African medical car driver Alan van der Merwe arrived on the scene. Grosjean was taken to hospital, and there was an 80-minute delay as repairs were made to the crash barriers he had smashed into. During the break, there was a sense disbelief as people struggled to come to terms with what they had just witnessed. TV replays were beamed across the globe on F1's world feed showing Grosjean's fiery brush with death, footage that was especially uncomfortable for the drivers on the grid to see. Ricciardo was particularly scathing in his post-race comments, explaining that he felt it was disrespectful to show, especially as drivers were preparing to get back into their cockpits. 'I don't want to comment too much on the race,' he said. 'I want to express my disgust and disappointment with F1. The way the incident of Grosjean was broadcast over and over, the replays, it was completely disrespectful and inconsiderate for his family, for all our families, watching. We are going to be racing again in an hour and every time we look at the TV it is a ball of fire and his car is cut in half. We can see that tomorrow. We don't need to see that today. They are playing with all our emotions, and I thought it was pretty disgusting.'

It was understandable. Hamilton had already won the title in what was an unusual season due to Covid-19 protocols that had asked a lot of the drivers. This was a dead-rubber race that provided a brutal reminder of the dangers inherent in motor sport. Hamilton was asked whether such an incident might make him consider stopping racing, and his reply was bluntly honest: 'I would be lying if I was to say "no". It is so important to respect the sport and the dangers that are there. I have been racing 27 years and I've seen … from a young kid to Jules Bianchi, and his experience. When I was nine, I saw a kid die on the same day I won a race, so I have always been aware of the dangers and the risks that I take. But for sure, as you get on later in life, you question it more than perhaps when I was in my early twenties. Today, I saw the accident and then I am also thinking, "Romain, jeez, he has a wife and kids." It is something he will have to think heavily on because it is a privilege to be able to do what we do but there is so much else in life and things to do beyond F1. It was a huge crash, and the safety reminds us of the job that has been done, but more needs to be done and we will continue to work on it. I don't have any fear and I am sure we will get back in and do what we do, but I am not thinking of stopping because of that, no.'

After Grosjean's smash, it was a fairly processional win for Hamilton as he chalked up another victory. But there was a nervy moment at the end for Norris. Pérez was running in third and looked nailed-on for a podium until he suffered an engine failure and his Racing Point car caught fire. An over-enthusiastic marshal ran across the live race track, narrowly avoiding Norris'

McLaren. It was similar to the incident that killed British racer Tom Pryce in 1977 when he was struck by a fire extinguisher that was being carried by a marshal. Norris was stunned to see the marshal enter the track without permission, and over the team's radio said: 'He's the bravest guy I've ever seen.' Norris later added: 'I panicked. It was the last thing I was expecting. The guy didn't look both ways before he crossed the road. It was all very dark, and he was wearing black, and all I could see was a bouncing fire extinguisher. It was a pretty crazy moment.' All of the action detracted from the fact that Norris finished the race in fourth place, missing out on the podium to Albon by three seconds.

The following week, Grosjean was back at the Bahrain track, but the burns to his hands made it impossible for him to race in the Sakhir GP, and he was replaced by Pietro Fittipaldi. There was another notable absentee as Hamilton was forced to pull out after testing positive for Covid-19. His enforced absence meant that Mercedes called up George Russell to fill in for him. It was the first time since his time in F2 that the Williams driver had been offered a competitive car and he seized his chance in qualifying with an excellent second place on the grid, missing out to Bottas on pole by just 0.026 seconds. Meanwhile, Norris was caught out by traffic and qualified down in fifteenth place, and a further engine penalty demoted him to nineteenth on the grid. However, he produced an excellent recovery drive to finish in tenth place, while Russell suffered a heart-breaking puncture and was unable to capitalise on his slot at the front of the grid and came home in ninth place.

At the seventeenth and final race of a pandemic-hampered season, there was a real sense of achievement that the sport had been able to return under such circumstances. The testing protocols had been vigorous but also necessary to ensure the races went ahead. It was crucial that the season went ahead, especially given the financial risks that many teams faced when the racing – and income – stopped at the start of the year. None more so than McLaren, where the rumoured wage cuts and redundancies had been hard on the team. The team's iconic factory in Woking was also put up for sale as demands dried up for McLaren sports cars. But finding a way through had been made easier by the positive results on track. The podium for Norris in Austria and Sainz in Monza had been the stand-out highlights, while the duo's relationship had clearly had a positive impact on the team.

At the finale in Abu Dhabi, Norris finished fifth and Sainz was sixth; enough to ensure the Woking team finished in third place in the constructors' championship. It was some achievement to beat the likes of works teams such as Ferrari and Renault, plus big-spending Racing Point. And the third place in the championship also meant that the team received a larger portion of the prize-money pot. At the same time, there was also the added bonus of fresh investment from US firm MSP Sports Capital, with some predictions valuing the deal to be worth £185 million. McLaren might have been losing one of their drivers to Ferrari, but the progress the team had made with Norris and Sainz had been encouraging. Their finances were looking healthier, and there was much to look forward to in 2021. They would be welcoming a seven-time race-winner in Daniel Ricciardo, plus they would be rekindling their engine partnership with Mercedes, who were considered to be producing the best engine in the sport.

A NEW TEAMMATE

The winter off-season is always a fascinating time to follow drivers on social media as it is the only way of getting updates on what they are up to. During the season, there are the press conferences and the drivers have very little down-time in between the races to do anything else, whereas in the winter, there is a block of time for them to effectively do what they want. At the end of 2020, fans were given updates as Hamilton spent his time skiing in the US, while other drivers documented their gym workouts as they got in shape for the onslaught of a new campaign. Norris decided to spend some time in Dubai on holiday, and given the lingering risk of contracting Covid-19, it was not the biggest surprise when McLaren announced on 6 January that he had in fact tested positive for the virus. There was obviously a sense of concern for his health, but there were also questions raised as to how it had happened in the first place, especially given the strict protocols that were still in place.

Nonetheless, the team explained that he had lost his sense of taste and smell during the break in Dubai and a subsequent test had come back positive. 'McLaren can confirm Lando Norris tested positive for Covid-19 yesterday in Dubai, where he is currently on holiday ahead of a planned training camp,' the team said. 'In line with local regulations, he is now self-isolating at his hotel for fourteen days. He is currently feeling well and reports no other symptoms.' The timing was such that it did not necessarily present any issues, for he still had enough time to serve the self-isolation period and get his fitness back in time for the preseason tests in Spain in early March.

Norris was not the only driver to test positive over the winter either. Leclerc became the fifth driver to catch the virus when he too returned a positive test at his home in Monaco having also just returned from a holiday in Dubai. 'I want to let you know that I have tested positive for Covid-19. I am regularly checked according to my team's protocols. Unfortunately, I learned that I have been in contact with a positive case and immediately went into self-isolation, notifying anyone I had contact with. A subsequent test I took has come back positive. I am feeling OK and have mild symptoms. I will remain in isolation in my home in Monaco in compliance with the regulations set by the local health authorities. Stay safe and take care,' he said on his Instagram. Hamilton, plus Stroll and Pérez, had previously tested positive for the disease, but the new cases meant that there were question marks as to whether the start of the 2021 season might have to be delayed, as was the case the previous year.

By the time the car launches came around in mid-February, it was pretty clear that F1 would be pressing ahead as normal. At McLaren's launch at the MTC, there was a big effort to focus on the team's new driver pairing of Ricciardo and Norris. Unusually, following the car's livery launch, both drivers took to a recording studio to produce a novelty song. The pair headed into the recording booth to perform a rap and they were later let loose on a set of drums and a bass guitar. The fans clearly loved it – it was obviously a bit of fun, but it also served to bring the two drivers together by playing off the fact that the two of them liked to have a laugh. By now, Norris' reputation as someone who did not take himself too seriously was well known, particularly on social media. Meanwhile, Ricciardo was well established as the paddock joker.

Alongside the livery launch and the song, there were also interviews as Norris was quizzed about how he felt heading into his third season in F1. He revealed that he had stopped eating pizza in an attempt to get in shape. It seemed that he was finally beginning to make serious changes to his diet to help him improve physically. 'I have tried to be more strict with certain things,' he said in a media session with UK journalists, 'whether that is with food and trying not to have a pizza as often. I can still have a little treat now and then, but it is also the physical side of it, too. Trying to do more in the gym because I struggle with that part of it. I know I am in F1, and I am in a very privileged position, but that doesn't matter because I can still struggle to go out on a run or go into the gym and lift weights. I struggle to motivate myself, so I have tried more things and pushed myself through moments that I hate because I know that good things come of it. I am better prepared physically because of it. I am trying to think outside the box and dedicating more time to work out what is good for me and push myself to the next level. A lot of it is a mental game. I have tried to understand myself a bit more to push myself to the next level.'

It was interesting to hear Lando speak so openly about the lifestyle changes he had made, but it also made it clear that he felt he had to step up even further now that he was going up against his new teammate Ricciardo, who had more experience and race wins under his belt. With his friend Sainz departed for Ferrari, it was now up to Lando to assert himself rather than simply sit back and let Ricciardo take over as McLaren's new top dog. So how would that relationship play out? 'I don't think the arrival of Daniel makes it any harder,' he replied when asked about the Aussie's arrival. 'I worked with Carlos and he is an extremely good driver and there are things Carlos is going to be better at than Daniel and vice versa. I don't believe Daniel is a big step above anything that Carlos has achieved so it doesn't change much for me. There is more pressure on him because he has been in F1 for longer and he has to come in and perform very well and that is what he is here to do with his experience. I am in that earlier phase of my career. I still need to perform very well. I am in my third year and there are no excuses for me any more. It is an opportunity to learn from someone different and with more experience. I think it is harder for someone to go against a much younger driver than it is for a younger driver going up against someone with more experience. I have more responsibility now than the past few years. There is more on me now to lead the team and areas we can improve. In many ways it is going to be the hardest season, but I am hoping for the best season, too. I am the guy with the experience at McLaren, so I need to take on that role and show how it is done and lead the team in the right direction. It is a big opportunity for me to take up that lead and I will work very hard.'

Writing in the *i*, Kevin Garside reflected: 'It is tempting to say Lando Norris is not a kid any more, then you notice a birth certificate stamped in 1999. Nevertheless, Norris is about to embark on his third season in Formula One alongside McLaren's new signing Daniel Ricciardo. If a teammate is the standard by which drivers are measured, Norris is facing his toughest year yet against a driver McLaren had been courting for the past three years.'

Ricciardo was confident about the upcoming season. He was about to embark on his eleventh season in F1 and was under no real pressure, given McLaren had not won a drivers' title since 2008 and had slumped to ninth in the constructors' championship in 2015. 'I feel like McLaren have done things to set themselves up for the rule changes,' he said in reference to the plans for 2022. 'The next era of F1 has the ability to turn the field around a little bit. Everything I have seen excites me about where McLaren is heading. I believe in the personnel. They have more backing and are doing what it takes to be a real contender.'

While much of the focus was on the potential for a new bromance between the two drivers, in a similar way to the dynamic between Norris and Sainz, Brown sensed that it would not all be laughs and jokes and that the pairing could be explosive on the track. Speaking at the car launch, he said: 'Everyone is expecting them to be a goofy odd couple but I am expecting more seriousness. They are both out to prove something. Daniel is at the stage of his career where he wants to fight for a world championship and Lando is no longer the "younger brother" of his teammate. They are both extremely fast and Daniel is very aggressive and I think they will be tough to each other on track. I think we are going to have to manage them on track. Carlos and Lando gave each other a lot of room when they raced but I think Daniel and Lando will be closer wheel-to-wheel. We might need to make sure that everyone races hard but also races clean. I do think we have the most exciting driver pairing both on the track and off it. They both have an energy and ambition that has made McLaren a youthful and energetic racing team.'

Indeed, some staff at McLaren were concerned about how Norris would react to losing Sainz and how he would cope going up against a ruthless Ricciardo, who was eager to show Red Bull and Renault what they were missing out on. 'When Carlos left, I think Lando got a bit nervous again,' Sefton explains, 'because he was a bit like, "Well, this guy's obviously won seven races. He's a known quantity, and he's got a really good reputation." I felt like Lando's confidence had grown so much over the two years he had with Carlos. When Carlos left and we signed Daniel, Lando was a bit like, "I've really got to step up." That was when I noticed that Mark, his manager, and Jon, his trainer, were building a positive environment by explaining that Norris had all the tools

and experience and should not be putting pressure on himself …
I used to call him kiddo, in fact I still do, but that was the time
when I thought this guy actually could be really good and it will
be really interesting to see the comparison. Some thought Dan
would just come in and absolutely smash him, but he didn't. You
could certainly see a change in Lando, just the way he carried
himself, the way he spoke, his whole demeanour. He was just so
much more confident in himself while being self-deprecating.'

Norris had reason to feel confident too. He had a solid
preseason test, as did Ricciardo, as McLaren looked to build
on the success of the previous year. The addition of Ricciardo
seemed to give the team a lift, while there was hope that the
Mercedes engine would provide the power and reliability
the team were missing with Renault. During preseason testing,
it was also interesting to see Red Bull's Max Verstappen set the
early pace, and there was a feeling that Hamilton and Mercedes
would have their work cut out in trying to stop the Dutchman
from winning his first title.

But despite the sense of confidence and the positive
preseason, there was still a feeling that Norris would struggle
up against Ricciardo – perhaps in the hope that the Australian
would rediscover his best form after suffering a dip at Renault.
Ahead of the season-opener in Bahrain, I spoke to former F1
driver David Coulthard and discussed how he thought Norris
would do with his new teammate. 'This is a great test for Lando,'
said Coulthard. 'In Carlos he had a quick teammate but also
one that was pretty easy-going, and part of knowing your
competitors is knowing your teammate. And with Daniel, he's
easy-going off track, but he is pretty ruthless on track and has
that racer's heart and edge, which we saw come out when he was
alongside Max and Seb. It will be a difficult time for Lando. But
it's also a great opportunity for him to step up and show he can
get his elbows out.'

In an interview with the *Evening Standard*, Zak Brown could not resist the temptation to dream. Having seen the likes of AlphaTauri and Racing Point win races in 2020, if there was half a chance McLaren were in contention for a win, they would do all they could to make sure it happened, he said, while conceding they would not be regular winners. 'In unusual circumstances, I'd say we have a chance,' he said, 'but to stick it on pole and lead a race, that's going to be reserved for Mercedes and Red Bull.' The article in the *Standard* went on to focus on how Brown had helped turn the team around, and the thinking behind why they had changed the team's livery from silver to orange. 'We have a very loyal fan base,' he continued. 'It's like Manchester United or the New York Yankees – they have so many passionate fans that when you don't perform you hear about it. That's not pleasant but it never put me off. With our headquarters, we've got a really cool Star Wars vibe and the whole Darth Vadar thing worked for us for a while, but we were a little bit dark and cold with the black and silver. It felt like we needed energy and engagement with the fans, so we focused on them, which is why we changed to papaya. So, we're still going with the Star Wars theme but it's more Luke Skywalker.'

Catching up with Norris in Bahrain for the first race of 2021, I was eager to not only talk about the new season, but to also ask him about his latest posts on social media showing how he had taken up drumming. Having caught the bug following the team's launch event, Norris had been having video lessons with One Direction drummer Josh Devine. It was a different pastime from gaming and streaming, and one in which he was able to unleash his creative side – and fortunately, he had not had any complaints from his neighbours. 'I have only once played late, around 9pm, but I try and play in the afternoon or the early evenings,' he said when I asked him. 'We aren't in joining houses, so I have a little bit of sound breathing room. It is good to have something different to focus on and I get to let loose and to get rid of some of the anger I always have, but it is good to learn something new. I did a lesson with Josh, and we streamed it on Twitch and he taught me a few things, that was pretty cool. It is just about trying to learn it and see the improvements in yourself. There are lots of things I always want to try and do, like learning to play golf. But I don't commit to it and do it properly. You just go out there and practise, but I don't get very far and I end up giving it up. I just want to learn something I can be good at. Singing was off the cards at an early stage! There is no way to get me better at that, so drumming was the next thing, and it has been good fun.'

We also spoke about Sainz's departure and Norris' new relationship with Ricciardo. Norris explained how he was keen to knuckle down and put in the effort. 'There has been a lot more emphasis on doing everything I can do for the best in myself and the best for the team,' he said. 'So there has been a lot more time spent on working in different areas … making sure everything is as good as it can be. There is certainly more focus from my side. There is now a sense I can lead things in the team. There is a bigger role I have to take on because of my experience with this team and Daniel cannot fill that. So that is my responsibility to lead that and drive the team on. It does not mean we are not going to laugh and have fun every now and again, because everyone does, but there is more focus this year.' On his aspirations for 2021, he was looking to add to the podium he took in Austria. Hailing the results in the Bahrain test, which followed the one in Barcelona, he described how 'the whole team are on top of things and looking at every area and improving where we possibly can' but that there was 'more to come from the car and the engine'.

The Bahrain GP proved to be an absolute thriller, as Hamilton battled with Verstappen for the 96th victory of his career in a race that would set the tone for the rivalry between the two drivers for the rest of the season. They raced hard over the 56 laps, but it was the final six that had the TV audience glued to their sets as Verstappen sized up an overtaking manoeuvre. He managed the move on lap 53, but in doing so he left the track and was ordered by the stewards to give the place back to Hamilton. At the second attempt, on the penultimate lap, he locked up, and in a flash, Hamilton was gone and on his way to victory. Afterwards, the Brit declared the win as 'one of the hardest races I've had for a while', with Verstappen in second and Bottas in third. The dramatic end to the race took the attention away from the driver who came home in fourth place: Norris. He delivered a faultless drive from seventh on the grid to narrowly miss out on the podium places. It was no fluke either. He was third in first practice and second in second practice as the preseason pace continued into the first grand prix. He was understandably delighted, not only with the decent start to the season, but he had also got the better of Ricciardo, who was placed in seventh.

At the Emilia-Romagna Grand Prix, news came that George Russell was looking to move to Monaco. The benefits of living by the Mediterranean are obvious in terms of lifestyle, while the tax advantages are also appealing to big-earning F1 drivers. But when the same question was put to Norris, he was again quite adamant that a switch from Woking to the Riviera was not on the cards any time soon. 'It is just having fun, being with my mates and seeing my family when I want and it is all easy and I enjoy that,' reported *The Times*. 'That's all I want at the moment, and I just want to live my life normally. If I moved to Monaco, I really would not enjoy it and I don't want to do my job in Formula One and not enjoy the things around it. That's why I am staying where I am.' The article did come to the conclusion that Lando could now definitely 'afford the move' given he was 'earning £4 million a year', while also pointing out that he had recently set up his own esports team, Quadrant, which was attracting considerable interest.

The Emilia-Romagna Grand Prix itself is a curious race. Held at the Autodromo Internazionale Enzo e Dino Ferrari, it is more widely known as Imola. The circuit is 40 kilometres from Bologna, and in March 2022, an agreement with F1 confirmed that the track would host the Emilia-Romagna Grand Prix until 2025. This was a serious commitment for a European race, especially given the small size of Imola's hospitality facilities and grandstands, and that the majority of the infrastructure is not a patch on modern F1 venues. However, there is a special connection between the circuit and Formula One, with CEO Stefano Domenicali having been born in Imola and spent weekends during his childhood watching cars race at the track. He would later help out in the paddock and media centre as he began his career in motor sport.

As a racetrack, Imola has a long history and will forever be associated with the two tragic crashes that killed Ayrton Senna and Roland Ratzenberger in 1994. The circuit held the San Marino GP between 1981 and 2006 but then fell off the F1 calendar. In 2020, during the Covid-19 hit season, Imola was chosen as one of the seventeen rounds, with the race being won by Hamilton on 1 November 2020.

The race, under the new name of the Emilia-Romagna Grand Prix, returned in 2021, but its 18 April date meant that weather conditions were cold and wet. Norris had shown good pace in the final practice session and was second behind Verstappen and ahead of Hamilton. But it was Hamilton who was on pole for the actual race with Pérez in second and Verstappen lining up in third. Meanwhile, Norris was down in seventh, one spot behind his teammate Ricciardo. But in the race, the Brit showed incredible calmness as he plotted his way around the wet track. There was a big shunt between Russell and Bottas, which saw the race stopped temporarily, while Hamilton also had a minor crash as he hunted down Verstappen. The Dutchman took the chequered flag, with Hamilton second, in a reversal of the season-opening result, but this time, Norris was third – going one better than he did in Bahrain. His second podium finish in his 40th F1 race – and on his own merit too, for there were no penalties to change the outcome of the top three. He'd done it completely on his own – and he was now third in the drivers' championship, a huge result given Ricciardo was sixth. But for the explosive nature of Bottas and Russell's crash, Norris' achievement would have been top billing for the headlines, not that it bothered him.

At the Portuguese GP that followed, Norris was fifth behind the two Red Bulls and the two Mercedes as he proved best of the rest. Ricciardo was a disappointing ninth, and by now, the narrative was clear: Norris was driving McLaren forward and was not going to be overshadowed or threatened by Ricciardo. 'He was fourth at the first race in Bahrain and in Imola he was third, so that's when we knew about Lando's confidence and it changed him,' recalls Sefton. 'At first, they were both definitely trying to suss each other out. We never thought they would not get on, but they just didn't spend any time together … There was never any animosity between them, it was just they didn't hang out. Andreas [Seidl – McLaren's former team principal] would have a meeting with both drivers before the race every Sunday. It's called a "pre-race objectives meeting" and he would basically lay the law down and tell both drivers they are in it together. You drive for the team, no driver is better than the other, no one gets preferential treatment, you do what's best for the team result, that kind of thing … Both drivers were team players and we needed that because we knew we were struggling and that Ferrari would be back up there again. Both of them then started spending more time together in engineering meetings and worked really hard on it. I can't fault either of them. Both their work ethics are just unbelievable … but they started to work together quite a lot and from then, their relationship started to change and they started to get on really well.'

After his excellent start to the season, Norris was rewarded with a new contract by McLaren in mid-May 2021, with the news broken by an emailed press release rather than an event. It came after the Spanish GP, where he finished eighth in an off weekend. Nonetheless, McLaren were keen to sign him up to a new contract that would fend off any interest from rival teams. After the opening four races, he was fourth in the drivers' championship and just six points behind Mercedes' Bottas. Norris' multi-year deal was rumoured to be worth around £6 million a year and saw him move to improved terms to reflect his position within the team. The press release quoted Norris saying: 'I'm really pleased to have extended my relationship with McLaren from 2022. Having been with the team for almost five years, I feel very much part of the family here and I couldn't imagine starting the next phase of my career anywhere else. McLaren has been a huge support since my days in junior series and I've really enjoyed learning and developing as a driver since. My commitment to McLaren is clear: my goal is to win races and become Formula One world champion and I want to do that with this team.' The quotes from Brown were fairly straightforward in what seemed to be a fairly routine amendment. 'I'm delighted with the extension of our agreement with Lando for 2022 and beyond,' said Brown. 'He's been instrumental in our return to form here at McLaren and we're proud of the growth he's shown since he first started with us back in 2017. Lando is one of the brightest talents on the Formula One grid and we look forward to seeing him continue to go from strength to strength both on and off track.'

The new contract came ahead of the Monaco GP, and before the race, Norris was in a bright mood when he was asked by reporters about the deal, saying that he wanted to become one of the team's leaders to drive the famous team back to the top step of the podium. 'I want to be that kind of guy who can lead the team,' he said in Monte Carlo, 'who has been there for many years, who has helped them through the bad times and helped them achieve the good times. And that's why I'm still here, that's why I signed for some more years, because I want to be in that position. Even this year I already took a step forward in that position. I'm feeling like a different and improved driver to the last couple seasons, taking on more responsibility and leading the team in more ways. So that's definitely something I like, something I want to be able to do going into the future.'

Interestingly, and in his own self-deprecating manner, Norris also revealed that he started the discussions with Brown about a renewal over dinner earlier in the year, and that it was a discussion that made him feel uncomfortable. 'As much as I want to win races and win championships and so on, the other thing that's just as important to me is making sure I enjoy where I am,' he explained. 'So just as much as winning and success means to me, actually having fun, enjoying my life is just as important. And that comes with the loyalty side of it, the same mechanics, the same engineers working with those people for many years and that's where I get a lot of that from. There's nothing more that I like than to continue being where I am. It was something I brought up when I went to dinner with Zak a while ago. He was talking a little bit about the future, and I was just like, "You know, about these future years, is it something we want to start talking about now? Is it something you want to talk about later in the season?" Just because I don't know when or how to bring it up, just like a guy talking to a girl for the first time, so it was a bit awkward because I've not been in that position before.'

However, the timing of the deal seemed to be perfect as Norris went on to take his third, and arguably his biggest, podium in F1 in Monaco.

It was a superb drive that required focus and skill as the result moved him into third place in the drivers' championship standings. His weekend had started well, after he qualified fifth on Saturday. He was promoted to fourth when Leclerc had a gearbox issue on the way to the grid. And during the race he moved up another place after Bottas, who had been running second, suffered a bungled pit stop as his Mercedes team failed to remove one of his tyres, forcing him to retire. Norris was then chased to the flag by Pérez in his Red Bull, as the Mexican pressed for a podium, but Norris held on to finish behind Verstappen and Sainz for third. 'It's a cool feeling,' Norris said after the race. 'You don't know how cool it is until you're actually there, it's incredible. It's a fricking long race, especially with Pérez the last few laps. I know you can defend relatively easily in Monaco but there's still just that pressure and seeing him in my mirrors every time I go round the corner is just a bit stressful. The Red Bull is a bit quicker than us, they were blatantly faster, but it's a track you can defend relatively easily on, as long as you've got them covered, then you're in good shape, so as long as I didn't make any mistakes there then I knew I'd be in with a good shot.' That said, it was not especially comfortable at the time, as he snapped at his race engineer, Will Roberts, to stop all radio communication so that he could focus.

Afterwards, he continued with his celebration as he was joined by Sainz on the podium. 'I'm super happy,' he said, '[a podium] is more special here in Monaco. I definitely didn't think we would get this coming into this weekend. We thought it would be one of the toughest [weekends] all season but it's almost turned into one of the opposites. It's pretty insane, pretty incredible. It feels amazing. It got to halfway [in the race] and I thought, "I have to do that again?" It's tough mentally to keep that focus, that concentration, but it paid off so it doesn't matter what you feel. It's all about the end result.' He later added: 'The trophy goes in the cabinet at McLaren, as always. But I will keep the presentation box because it is the coolest thing, a bespoke Louis Vuitton number. I will also make sure I get a replica of the trophy.'

Not only was there the new contract to accompany the win, but McLaren were also running a special one-off Gulf livery for the weekend, taking on the oil company's famous blue and orange colour scheme. All in all, it was a pretty perfect weekend, although not for Ricciardo, who was lapped by Norris and finished twelfth.

But for his poor race in Monaco, Ricciardo's involvement in the team was having a positive impact on Norris. He had already won over his engineers and mechanics with his stints in the garage post-race, helping them clear up and complete the packing before heading off to the next race. But he was now fully integrated into the team.

'Daniel's arrival was a really positive thing for Lando because it helped him to integrate more within the team,' says Sefton. 'He had worked with the boys for a long time by now, but he knew everyone, not just them by name, but their girlfriends, their wives, their kids, their families, their situation. He'd take the team out bowling or for dinner. I think he really understood the value of trying to galvanise people around him and that made him part of the furniture.'

Norris continued to show consistent speed and results. In the Azerbaijan Grand Prix, the French Grand Prix at Paul Ricard and the Styrian Grand Prix at the Red Bull Ring in Austria, he was fifth in all three races. The only negative was that had it not been for the stewards' decisions, he would have had an even better return of points. In Baku, Norris' chances were limited when he received a three-place grid penalty for Sunday's race that left him 'gutted' and more than a little upset at the penalty points placed on his racing licence. The incident occurred when he crossed the start-finish line after the red flag had come out for Antonio Giovinazzi's crash in the first segment of qualifying. Norris was preparing to start a flying lap when the red flag came out but did not have enough time to safely make the pit-lane entry. He asked his team whether he should pit, but the reply was to land and he stayed out on track rather than change for fresh tyres. By crossing the start line, he triggered a breach of the rules and a subsequent penalty, which was reduced from a five-place grid drop to three, with the stewards acknowledging he had 'only a very short time to react'.

Norris gave a positive response to a question posed to him about Russell's future, as he was now enjoying his shot at a front-running team, while Russell struggled at Williams. 'I rate George a lot,' said Norris ahead of the French Grand Prix when he was asked about the future of his fellow Brit', 'he is one of the best – and I think he will give Hamilton a hard time. It is too early to tell if he is as good as Lewis. However, he is an extremely good driver. He is in his comfort zone at the moment, he is the main guy in his team – he is sitting so comfortably and can do what he wants. But we also saw in Bahrain last season when he got put in that Mercedes, he was pretty much ahead of Bottas for the whole race. He should have finished ahead and won the race, so I don't expect anything less after those performances from last season. He is very fast and he will give Lewis a hard time. I would love to see George there [at Mercedes]. I am sure he will have a chance, everyone knows it. It is just a matter of when, rather than if. A British rivalry would be exciting as well.

He is a good friend. We have grown up racing together and we get along.'

However, it was Russell's future Mercedes teammate that was on Norris' mind for much of the Austrian Grand Prix, as he posted his fourth podium finish. He had impressed by qualifying in second place – a career best at that point – but it was his drive during Sunday's race that would earn him some widespread recognition. For an early part of the race, Hamilton had loomed large in Norris' mirrors as he pursued the McLaren man in the hope of pressuring him into making a mistake. But lap after lap, Norris covered off the threat from Hamilton, who radioed his team saying, 'Such a great driver, Lando.' It was unusual to say the least. We frequently hear from drivers who are agitated about a rival's driving, but rarely do we hear them praising their competitors, especially in the heat of battle.

The race was won by Verstappen with Bottas in second and Norris in third, but the young Brit was not happy about the result and was again left feeling hard done by. This was because he was served another penalty, for forcing Pérez off the track, landing him with a five-second forfeit, without which he would have been second. He picked up the penalty on the fourth lap and on the first lap after a safety car restart. Pérez had tried to pass Norris around the outside but the McLaren driver held his ground, resulting in the Red Bull running wide into the gravel. While Norris served his penalty in a pit stop, he lost track position to Bottas and was unable to regain P2. 'It was exciting, but I'm disappointed,' he said after the race, 'because we should have been in second place. I thought that lap was just racing really. He tried to go around the outside, which is a bit stupid, and he ran off the track himself. I didn't even push him, so I don't know. I'm frustrated but also happy with P3. We had very good pace.' Even Red Bull boss Christian Horner had some sympathy for Norris. 'I didn't have a major problem with the

Lando move,' Horner told Sky Sports. 'It was racing. It was hard racing. It was wheel-to-wheel. That's racing. Otherwise, you're going to get drivers just chucking themselves off the circuit and claiming penalties. So it's a bit disappointing. For me, that's hard racing.'

Norris' frustration aside, it was Hamilton's gushing praise that drew the attention of the media, with Norris admitting the flattery had given him a boost in confidence. 'It was cool hearing it from Lewis,' he admitted, 'more so than from any other driver in F1. It was in the middle of the race, which I wouldn't ever do. And it was a bit odd because you don't expect to hear it. But it means even more that he said it after he had gone past, and I was racing against him, rather than him dropping back because of any problems. So it was weird but cool at the same time because it was the first time I'd ever raced against Lewis for more than one corner. You know he's the best. And he's the best for a reason. He's good at attacking and defending, but I feel like I was capable of holding him off for twenty laps. Now I know that, if I'm in the same position next time, I'm able to do it. In the past it's been the case where, after lap five, I'm thinking, "Oh no." But if the speed difference is the same, I'm more confident knowing I can keep him behind me.'

After his podium in Austria, it was a bit of a shock to see Norris on daytime TV in the UK as a guest on *This Morning*, with presenters Phillip Schofield and Holly Willoughby. It was his first appearance on the programme, but it would prove to be an important platform for him in the months to come.

On the Monday afternoon ahead of the British Grand Prix, Norris walked into a boardroom at the MTC. He was there for some media interviews in the run-up to his home race. He was in a relaxed mood and was asked about his weekend as he had posted images from Wembley where England had lost the Euro 2020 final to Italy in a tense penalty shootout after the game had finished 1–1 at the end of extra time. Norris shared pictures of himself attending the match on his personal Instagram account and posted the message, 'Proud of our team' on his story. He said it was his first ever football match and that it was a 'pretty cool one to be able to get to'. There was not even the slightest hint that something had gone wrong after the match as journalists proceeded to ask him about how he felt about racing in front of more than 140,000 people at Silverstone in the coming weekend. He was attracting plenty of fans and was sitting fourth in the drivers' championship with three podiums in the season. Norris admitted that his upturn in form was largely down to his fitness and nutrition work. 'I definitely run a lot more now,' he said. 'At the Red Bull Ring I went for a run every day. I definitely do more things than what I've done in the past. I still hate it with a massive passion but I know I've got to do it. It's all part of doing better this year. It's not just that I'm driving better because I'm just driving better. It's because of the work I do here because of my nutrition and my eating and my training and things making sure I'm at the top of every level that I can be.'

Soon after departing the MTC, I learned that there was in fact something Norris, and McLaren, had understandably not been keen to speak about. By that evening, the news had been confirmed in a statement. Upon exiting Wembley Stadium after the England match, Norris had been targeted by muggers, who robbed him of his watch as he went to get into his McLaren. The team's statement confirmed that Norris had been left 'shaken' by the experience. It said: 'McLaren Racing can confirm that Lando Norris was involved in an incident after the Euro 2020 final match at Wembley, during which the watch he was wearing was taken. Thankfully, Lando was unharmed but he is understandably shaken. The team is supporting Lando and we are sure that racing fans will join us in wishing him all the best for the British Grand Prix this weekend.' The statement added that no further comment would be made 'as this is now a police matter'. The attack in itself was headline news, with a lot of media focusing on the fact that the watch in question was a bespoke item from the team's sponsor, Richard Mille, and was said to be worth £40,000.

It was not until a few days later at Silverstone for the Thursday media sessions that it was possible assess the impact the incident was having on Norris. The relaxed figure that was in the MTC on Monday had become more subdued as the enormity of the attack, plus the overwhelming support he had received for being a victim in this unfortunate event, had started to sink in. The adrenaline rush from the shock had now dissipated and left behind a nervousness and a sense of vulnerability. 'I'm not in perfect condition, I'm not going to lie,' he said in the paddock. 'I have some work to do, mentally. Of course, I talk about that a lot and mental health, and mental strength is very important, but I've not been sleeping that great, and so on. It is not ideal and I'm feeling a bit sore. But I'm not the guy in the worst position after Wembley. I'll work on it, I'll make sure I'm in the best shape possible and I feel like I can still go out and focus on what I need to do and that's the main thing. It was not the night I wanted, and I guess not the night we all wanted from an England perspective and definitely not the way I wanted it to end. It's not the nicest experience for anyone to go through and it's not only me that it's happened to, it's happened to other people. It's something I don't wish upon anyone and of course if anyone else goes through it, I can sympathise with them and I know what they feel like.' While Norris had no lasting physical injuries, it was clear from his comments that the mugging had caused other issues that were not visible, but Brown and the team were trying to be supportive in any way they could. 'I guess the team did not want it all to be widely known after the incident happened,' explains Sefton. 'I messaged him and said I was so sorry and obviously heard that there was a police report because of the missing watch and the insurance claim. When I saw him when he came to the factory, he was really subdued, and I just gave him a hug and I asked him if he wanted to talk me through it and he just said it happened so fast. I think because he had lived a fairly sheltered life, nothing like that had ever happened to him before. I remember when he walked in, he was worried because he thought he was going to be in trouble because of the watch getting stolen.'

Despite the terrible incident, Norris put aside his ordeal to post a fifth-place finish in the sprint race, as F1 tried a new format for the race weekend in the hope of spicing up the action. The 100-kilometre race on the Saturday was also used to determine the grid for Sunday's actual grand prix, where Norris finished in fourth place. The race was won by Hamilton, while Leclerc was second and Bottas third, but all the talk afterwards was about Hamilton's first-lap crash with Verstappen, which sent the Red Bull into the barriers and required him to be sent to hospital for further checks. The fall-out was bitter between the two drivers and their respective team bosses and set the tone for the remainder of the season. Unsurprisingly, the feud had dominated the news agenda, and Norris' achievement did not get the coverage it deserved. Nor did the fact he had paid tribute to key workers and the NHS with a helmet designed specifically for the race. Taking advantage of the change in rules that permitted drivers to alter their helmet designs as many times as they like during the season, Norris' helmet featured handwritten messages from his fans, gathered via his social media accounts. 'From us, to you: Thanks Key Workers,' Norris wrote on Twitter before revealing that he would be raffling off the helmet to raise money for Our

Frontline, a charity that provides mental health support for frontline workers.

Norris left Silverstone in third place in the drivers' championship, and it was a place he would find himself at the midway point of the season after the Hungarian Grand Prix, despite retiring from the race in Budapest. Norris was caught up in a collision with Bottas and the damage caused by the Finn was sufficient to see them both fail to finish. Curiously, it was the eleventh race of the season and made an unwelcome hat-trick of sorts for the Brit. In his previous two years in F1, he had suffered a DNF in the eleventh race of that season. The 2019 German Grand Prix and the 2020 Eifel Grand Prix – the Hungarian Grand Prix completed the set.

The summer break was a good time to reflect on how much progress Norris had made. Physically, he had changed from when he first arrived in F1. When he made his debut, his complexion was that of a teenager, and his physique was that of a boy. But there had been a noticeable change as he sat in the paddock at the Hungaroring; he was tanned and his biceps were beginning to poke out from underneath his white McLaren polo shirt. His plans for his summer break were clear, 'I will go and see a few friends on holiday and enjoy the sun,' he said. 'Just have some time away but I will stay away from computers. I realise how much better it is for me to get outside. Playing golf and doing things like that makes life better away from Formula One. I used to take my PlayStation everywhere and my laptop but now I just take a book. Something I never thought I'd say. I realised the importance of going out for dinner with my friends. I still find it enjoyable playing the games but I've stopped taking life for granted and started enjoying it more. There is still a kid inside of me because I love games yet my mentality has changed.' Now he was over his ordeal at Wembley, he was also able to reflect on the popularity he experienced at Silverstone, with fans dressed in

McLaren clothing bearing his name or even from his Quadrant gaming range. 'It is an awesome feeling to see people now wearing my clothing range,' he reflected in Budapest. 'It makes me smile because I know they like me but it is weird because when I was growing up I never thought about being in that position.'

HEARTBREAK IN RUSSIA

When the season resumed at the Belgian GP, it proved to be one of the most farcical races in decades, but more importantly for Norris, it was a race for which he was lucky to escape with his life. Qualifying took place in torrential rain with conditions so bad that some drivers even radioed their team's to provide feedback to the FIA's race director, Michael Masi, to stop the race. Poor visibility coupled with a lack of grip, and memories of the tragic death of Hubert on the same Spa track in 2019, meant that it was perfectly reasonable that requests were made to red flag the session. However, without such intervention from the stewards, it was inevitable that the drivers would be taking risks as they continued to push for better lap times.

This proved to be the case for the McLaren driver, who lost control of his car at 185 mph, travelling up the famed Eau Rouge section of the track, close to where Hubert lost his life. Norris smashed into the barriers and, as had been the case in the fatal F2 smash, the car was expelled back onto the track, spinning 360 degrees four times. Norris was fortunate that there were no cars immediately behind him, for he would certainly have been struck. As his team in the garage held their heads in concern, his race engineer asked: 'Are you OK?' Breathing deeply, Norris, who had topped the timing screens in Q1 and Q2 and could have taken pole, replied: 'Yeah, sorry, guys, we were on for a good one.' He was helped out of his cockpit by marshals, holding his left arm awkwardly before he stepped into the medical car. He was taken to hospital for a precautionary scan on his arm. Only moments before the incident, Vettel had urged Masi to stop the session, and when he learned of Norris' accident, he was fuming: 'What did I fucking say? Red flag. It's unnecessary!' He later added: 'I think Michael is not proud of what happened. It is always easy to play "Captain Hindsight", but we need to find a way to listen more to the information that we have from around the track.'

Late on Saturday night, a McLaren spokesperson confirmed that Norris had been cleared to race on Sunday. Meanwhile, Norris posted a message on his Instagram thanking his fans for the messages of support, adding: 'Big crash and feeling a little bruised but I'm well and recovering ready for the race tomorrow.'

The wet weather continued the following day and, with Norris needing new parts and therefore taking a grid penalty, he lined up fifteenth. Not that it mattered, for having learned his mistake the previous day, Masi decided not to gamble with the conditions. After over three hours of delays and suspended starts, the Grand Prix started at 6.17pm local time but lasted for one lap from the pit lane and two further laps behind the safety car. The pitiful running at reduced speed constituted enough for the race to be classified and half-points were awarded for the top ten. However, the embarrassing scenes and lack of racing had made the sport look silly, and those fans at the track petitioned for a refund for their tickets.

The 2021 Italian Grand Prix would live long in the memory for McLaren – and even longer for Zak Brown, who had the iconic track layout tattooed on his arm following the team's unexpectedly successful weekend. In an explosive race that would feature another huge crash between the two championship rivals, Ricciardo was on hand to capitalise and went on to win McLaren's first race since the 2012 Brazilian Grand Prix. It was a remarkable achievement made even sweeter by Norris taking second place, as the team finished one-two for the first time since the 2010 Canadian Grand Prix.

The race was the second time that F1 had used the sprint race weekend format to determine the grid for Sunday's race. It was Verstappen and Hamilton who dominated practice before Bottas and Norris entered the mix during qualifying. The McLaren driver qualified in fourth, behind the other three drivers for the sprint race, which itself was a dull procession after some first-lap drama that saw Hamilton drop places and Ricciardo make it up to third at the expense of Norris, who finished in fourth place. Bottas' joy at his victory in the sprint was soon tempered by the grid penalty he took for an unscheduled engine change. As a result, he was dropped down to nineteenth for the start of the GP, promoting all those behind him up by one place. Consequently, Ricciardo would start second, behind Verstappen, who was now in P1, and Norris was bumped up to third on the grid.

If the sprint was a procession, Sunday's race was anything but. Ricciardo beat Verstappen off the line, while Hamilton passed Norris into third. Hamilton then tried to pass Verstappen but was squeezed wide, causing him to drop back behind Norris again. A problem for Verstappen in the pits allowed Norris to move into second place, while Hamilton's slow stop put him side-by-side with the Red Bull man when he came out of the pit lane. The two were wheel-to-wheel going into the first corner. Neither gave way and the pair banged wheels, launching Verstappen's car into the air and over the top of the Mercedes. The collision put both cars out of the race, despite Hamilton's attempts to get moving again – the additional weight of the Red Bull on top of him proved too difficult to shift.

The already bitter rivalry between the two championship leaders was cranked up another notch, with both drivers refusing to take responsibility. Hamilton later commented that he was lucky to be alive as the tyre of the Red Bull came close to striking his head. The halo cockpit canopy protection system that had protected Grosjean had saved another driver from potential harm. Ricciardo capitalised on the chaos and was able to win his first race since the 2018 Monaco Grand Prix. Afterwards, he was incredibly emotional given the pressure he was putting himself under to try and turn his form around. It was clear that he had been harbouring lots of pent-up negativity from his time at Renault and that he was also disappointed to be trailing to his new teammate at McLaren.

After the race, he made the following statement: 'It means everything. I definitely try not to make, or dictate, my life happiness around the sport because it's been three and a half years since I won so I'd be pretty miserable most of the time if I just based my happiness on winning races. Deep down I never lost faith or the belief and I think I needed to step back and that's where I think having some time off in August helped, and I truly think that helped this weekend, to get to this position. It feels reassuring for me. I believe in myself; I think everyone does to get to this point in the sport. I've certainly been challenged this year and the sport is a tricky one. It's not so black and white and sometimes you do struggle to find some answers. But you have to stay true to the course and you can easily get lost as well. Deep down I would have moments of frustration or moments of dropping my head but I kind of made a point never to let that last. For moments you fall out of love with the sport, but actually the clarity you get afterwards makes you realise how much you do love it and how much you want it. That's the biggest thing this weekend, that I knew I'd have a chance to fight for a podium and, yes, the want shone through and when it gets to that point and that level, I'll back myself to the hilt.'

However, it could have been a very different story had Norris overtaken the Australian. At some points of the race, Norris radioed his team urging them to ask Ricciardo to pick up the pace. Team orders are a key part of F1, despite being unpopular, especially among fans who want to see drivers race flat out in a battle to the line. But with teams being global corporations with shareholders, and employing thousands of staff, getting the result for the team is what matters most. Norris clearly felt he was quicker than Ricciardo and wanted permission to overtake. However, unlike some drivers who decide to take matters into their own hands, Norris respected the instruction not to overtake Ricciardo, even though it meant that he was denied the chance to win his first F1 race. As he crossed the line, Norris' radio message was one of sheer delight for the team. 'Let's go, boys!' he shouted. 'Yes boys! We deserved that. I am proud of the whole team, thanks for all your hard work. Congrats to Dan and that side of the garage too.' He was genuinely pleased for his teammate, despite wanting so desperately to break his duck.

'We thought we could be on for a right result,' explained Sefton when I asked her about that victory. 'Because Daniel had done well in the sprint, we thought we might be able to sneak a podium and then what happened in the race, we watched in disbelief. It felt like the longest hour and 45 minutes of my entire life. I've never known such a nervous ball of energy as the atmosphere inside the garage. We were all looking at the screens and could not believe what was happening. And then Lando came on the radio saying, "I think I'm faster" and "how's the position looking?" The team was like, "hold position, hold position". I didn't want Lando to push because I thought we cannot risk this. We've got to just hold fire and he did. And actually, he was really gracious. And I think he was sad that it wasn't him who got it, but at the same time, he understood the importance and how much this meant to the whole team. After the race, we went back to the Hilton and the staff had put up a banner saying congratulations and all the staff were applauding us when he got back. The team put some money behind the bar and everyone had a drink. Everyone felt it was important for us to have that time, as the team had deserved it.'

The mood could not have been more different following the next race in Sochi as Norris saw another victory slip through his fingers in the harshest of circumstances. The 2021 Russian Grand Prix will go down in the history books as Hamilton's 100th victory in F1, but that is not the full story. Norris had taken pole position as he utilised slick tyres on a drying track, which allowed him to set the quickest time on the Saturday. It was his first ever pole position and in doing so he became the 102nd driver to achieve the feat. It was also McLaren's first pole position since the 2012 Brazilian Grand Prix. Fittingly, his former teammate Sainz was second, while Russell was an unlikely third for Williams, as no Mercedes or Red Bull driver made it into the top three, with Hamilton crashing during qualifying and Verstappen choosing not to run as he would already be starting at the back of the grid due to engine penalties.

The Russian Grand Prix is often fairly dull as the track does not lend itself to great racing. The 53 laps can sometimes turn into a bit of a procession, so tyre management is all-important and drivers are required to eke out as much life as possible from their rubber to ensure they pit at the right time. Strangely, no non-Mercedes driver has ever won the race, which even includes the two grand prix held in 1913 and 1914. The Mercedes team won all eight races held between 2014 and 2021, with Hamilton, Bottas and Nico Rosberg all taking the chequered flag.

At the start, Sainz was able to pass Norris into Turn Two, while Hamilton quickly dropped back to sixth. The McLaren man did regain the lead on lap thirteen when he overtook Sainz, but then Hamilton started cutting his way through the field. Norris started to come under pressure from the world champion as the final few laps of the race started to get interesting, especially when it started to rain around lap 47.

The bad weather had been forecast but Norris was so focused on keeping Hamilton behind him, he missed the calls of his team asking him to pit. Kimi Räikkönen, Russell and Bottas were the first to come in for intermediate tyres, which offered better grip in the wet than the slicks. Verstappen, Ricciardo and Sainz all did the same in the deteriorating conditions. Norris knew full well that if he could nurse his car to the end he would win his first F1 race. The memory of seeing Riccardo take his victory was still fresh in his mind, so Norris knew that the car was good enough. The wet weather proved too much for Hamilton, who decided to pit for intermediate tyres on the advice of his team. It was painful to watch Norris as he slipped off the track a number of times, doggedly going against the advice from the pit wall, even though he had a 50-second gap over third place. He was adamant he could make it to the end, while Hamilton was 25 seconds behind when he made his pit stop. He just needed to stay out of danger, but by now it was fully raining, and he was forced to slow for every corner. As Norris' speed dropped, Hamilton sliced into his slender advantage. The gap had closed from 25 to two seconds with three laps to go when Norris' luck finally ran out and he aquaplaned off the track, allowing Hamilton to pass and take the win. The agony was felt in living rooms across the world. Even Hamilton could not help but feel some sympathy for Norris, who eventually finished the race in seventh place, and received a reprimand from the stewards for a pit lane infringement right at the death.

'Russia was just the worst ever,' says Sefton. 'Lando got that pole and we were like, "What the hell has happened in these last few weeks?" Lando was just feeling really confident and while he was so happy with pole, I don't really think we ever thought we'd get the win. He was leading the race and then the rain fell. It felt like the slowest time of my entire life, like watching a slow train crash.'

Formula One managing director Ross Brawn hailed Norris' weekend in his column for F1.com, picking him as his Driver of the Day. Brawn, who famously masterminded Schumacher's career, said that there comes a time when drivers should ignore their team's instructions and drive with their gut instinct, as Norris had done by not pitting for intermediate tyres. And while Brawn did say that it obviously turned out to be the wrong decision, he was confident that Norris would now become a better driver as a result of the experience. He wrote: 'Lando is my Driver of the Day. Listening to him on the radio when the team were talking to him, his composure was impressive. He's come on leaps and bounds in the last couple of years. Lando will be hurting right now. We all felt his pain when he slid off the track. It was a tragedy. I've been in that situation – when you need to make a big strategy call. I've won races by hanging on, I've lost races by hanging on … Those scenarios are so difficult and in Sochi it was especially tricky as only half the track was wet. Even with radar, no one is completely certain how wet it will be. And if you're leading a race, you don't want to give it up. When you're in the front, the guy in second has a much easier decision to make as he has nothing to lose. He either stays out and does what the guy in front does or takes a punt and he is unlikely to be any worse off than he was to begin with.

'Lando will go away from this and become a stronger driver. So much would have been preying on his mind, including the fact he managed to cope in qualifying better than anyone else. I see why he was insistent with his team. You could ask – should his McLaren team have taken the lead and insisted he pit when he said he didn't want to? A driver is in a bubble. He doesn't see what's going on. In this case, I'd say it's 60/40 in favour of the team making the decision but it's so difficult because you don't want to give up the lead of the race. That sinking feeling a driver or a team gets when they realise they made the wrong call, and the lead is evaporating before their very eyes, is horrible. They have my sympathies, but that kind of drama is what makes F1 so fantastic.'

A few days later, Norris was back in London in front of the cameras on *This Morning*. He was sat dressed in black next to his McLaren race car in the studio. He was asked an opening question about how he spent his free weekend, as the TV interview fell between the Russian and Turkish races, to which he said: 'After the last one? Crying … I normally have a few days reviewing and then a couple of days preparing for the next weekend.' Naturally, the quip was picked up on and he was asked about what had happened in Russia. By now, the dust had settled, and he had come to terms with the outcome, even if he stopped short of accepting full responsibility for failing to stop to change his tyres. 'It is a joint call. They [the team] need my input but I also need their input to make the right decision, and from what I was told, I made the call which I thought was best at the time. Little did we know, or what we should have known, was that there was a lot more rain coming and that decision was the wrong one. At the same time, it could have not rained as much and I'd have looked like a hero and won the race! But that's the way it goes. I want to say I still have a long career ahead of me, I hope, so in a way it is nice to get it done so that when these kinds of things come up again next time, I will be in a much better position.'

Norris was then asked if he'd been consoled by other drivers. 'Lewis did,' he explained, 'he was the one who effectively took the win from me, and that coming from Lewis – because he was the guy I watched growing up and to hear what he had to say – because he has been through many scenarios, it means something more.'

In the final part of the interview, Norris was asked about mental health and McLaren's partnership with the mental health charity Mind. He had spoken about mental health in the past, and earlier in the season he had addressed F1's growing race calendar and explained how double-headers and triple-headers were putting additional pressure on staff. In an interview in the *Guardian*, he had said: 'We don't talk about mental health as much as we should – and we really should. F1 are doing more and more and they are going down the right path but 23 races is not a help towards that. Twenty-three races is tough. The amount of racing is the only thing which can start to impact and take a toll on the team because they don't get to see their families much … For me that is one of the biggest things.'

This time, the presenters asked about Norris' own mental health and about him being unique in his willingness to address the subject in the first place. 'I was not always good at it and doing this,' he said, 'I am not confident doing it but I have realised over the three years how I can influence and impact people all over the world. What makes me happy is seeing other people smile and be happy. So the more I can do that and the more I can help them, then the messages I receive on social media always bring a smile to my face.'

Eighteen months later, Norris was interviewed by *GQ* and was again asked about mental health. He revealed that after his TV appearances and initially speaking out on the taboo subject, he was messaged by several who were inspired to seek help for their own struggles. 'A few people said that I had saved their life,' he is quoted in the magazine. 'That hits you pretty hard. It was a choice [to speak about mental health] because I struggled quite a bit with it in 2019 and 2020. I just didn't know how to deal with it. I kept all of it inside and it really hurt my self-belief and self-confidence, which got to an all-time low. I doubted myself: "Am I good enough to be in Formula One? Can I come back from this?" You're never going to please everyone. There are people that support you and people that don't. I know I'm doing the best I can.'

He was unaware at the time, but the Russian Grand Prix signalled the final time that McLaren would be in the hunt for wins that season. Top-ten finishes in Turkey, Austin, Mexico, São Paulo and Qatar had seen Norris replaced in the drivers' championship by Bottas and Pérez, as the Red Bull versus Mercedes battle hotted up. In the team's battle too, Ricciardo's form failed to improve following his victory in Monza, and Ferrari had now moved into third place in the constructors' championship.

Ahead of the Saudi Arabian Grand Prix, an unexpected email came from McLaren inviting me and a handful of other journalists for a catch up with Norris in London in November. Normally, the only access journalists get to drivers is when someone has a new sponsorship deal, a new contract or is planning to retire. As far as I was aware, there was no new sponsorship endorsement in the pipeline, and Lando had only signed a new deal just six months earlier. There was no sponsorship announcement due from McLaren, and retirement could definitely be ruled out.

The invitation was for a 1:30pm lunch at a high-end American steakhouse in Covent Garden, and when I arrived in the private room set aside for us with one big oval table, Lando was already there chatting with some of my fellow journalists. He was dressed casually in a hoodie and jeans and was clearly relaxed about the final few races of the season, despite the unknown of the new track in Saudi Arabia.

As the conversation was switched to on the record, we spoke about how Lando had enjoyed a fantastic season going up against his experienced teammate Ricciardo, plus the agony of missing out on his first win at the Russian Grand Prix, which still stung two months on.

But midway through the lunch, somewhere between the soup starters and the steaks, McLaren's excellent chief communication officer Tim Bampton interjected to reveal that Lando had some news he wanted to share with us.

As the waiter did his best to carry on his duties around the table, our eyes all flashed back to Norris, and he broke the news that he was moving to Monaco. It was a surprise, given he'd always spoken about the benefits of staying in the UK and living in his house in Addlestone close to McLaren's HQ. He was close to his mates, golf courses and, of course, his family home was within easy reach. Norris had previously stated that being near McLaren allowed him the opportunity to spend extra time on the team's simulator to prepare for races. There was no doubt that his late-night driving sessions in the factory impressed the McLaren bosses, but it also crucially allowed him to learn the F1 tracks, which was especially helpful in his first two seasons. But those factory visits also did not go unnoticed by staff. F1 is a team sport, and drivers rely on those employees in the factory to do a good job as much as the person changing the front-right wheel in a pit stop. They could see Norris was going the extra mile and in turn showed a willingness to learn and work hard.

However, having secured his place in the team and tied up his future, Norris felt that the benefits of living in Monaco outweighed those of living near the factory. He delivered the news in typical fashion – with a wry sense of humour that showed his maturity and how far he had come in terms of engaging with members of the media. 'I'm moving to Monaco after [the final race in] Abu Dhabi for the reasons you probably expect,' he explained. 'It's something that obviously a lot of drivers go to do, and especially with how racing is – I think you've seen it with a lot of the drivers, how quickly things can also go downhill. I still have to look after my life and things for my future so that's why I had to make the decision.' Without actually referring to the obvious tax benefits of moving to Monaco, Lando had conveyed the real reason behind the move. The principality is a haven for F1 drivers past and present. Of the current grid, Hamilton, Verstappen, Albon, Leclerc, Ricciardo and Bottas are all residents.

'I went with my managers and my trainer and we had a little look around a few different apartments and stuff,' he added. 'I was like, "I don't want to be in the same place as Max!" I don't know where Lewis is? He's on the opposite side … I don't know anybody else over there. But I'm around that area in Fontvieille, which is a nice, quiet place.' But it was also not an easy decision for Norris, who had made no secret of the fact he liked living in Woking. So, while the lure of the Côte d'Azur was obvious, it was certainly a decision that had taken him some time to make. Reflecting on weighing up the relocation, he said: 'Whenever I had a bad weekend, I could just go in on whatever day to be on the simulator to try things, speaking to my engineers, and so on. And I love England. It's still probably my favourite place to be. My family are there, my friends are there. And I said many times that for me, fun and enjoyment, and enjoying what I'm doing, takes priority over making these kinds of decisions. So, it's not a not an easy decision. And it's not something I've been thinking of for many years. I just feel like I'm in a comfortable place at the minute to make this decision and spend the time to move over there. I can still see a lot of my friends, and my family are going to come over.'

His uncertainty in making the decision was understandable. When Hamilton moved from the UK to Switzerland in 2007, he was heavily criticised for the move – and still is. There are further parallels too. Like Norris, Hamilton was 22 when he left the UK. He was also driving for McLaren.

Hamilton initially said his decision to move was down to a lack of privacy at home and he wanted to escape the public's gaze. At the time, he failed to mention the tax break he would enjoy living in Switzerland, which became a stick that people continue to beat him with.

When asked about whether he expected to receive criticism for the move, Norris was honest: 'Of course I'll understand and there's going to be some for sure, but people do many things in life for money. This is just another one.' He had mentioned the m-word, which made his reasoning obvious. The quotes were reported by the press, and sure, social media trolls were quick to jump in with the criticism, but Lando had largely avoided any controversy by breaking the news honestly and openly. And with the epic title fight between Hamilton and Verstappen dominating the news agenda, he was able to get his message out without too much negative attention. It proved to be a smart move all round.

The other notable conversation that day surrounded Lando's blossoming relationship with Portuguese model Luisinha Oliveira. It was the first time he had admitted to the media that he was seeing her, but he was keen for us to keep it quiet. We didn't know at the time, but he was flying off to see her after our lunch. Given the lengths his fans go to on social media to find out more about him, it was understandable that Norris wanted to keep the relationship private for the time being. He told a story of how he posted a photo on social media a few days after hitting some golf balls at a driving range. He had delayed making the post through fear of being pounced upon mid-bucket of balls. Oliveira had also been subjected to an extreme level of scrutiny after she posted a picture of an ice cream dessert, which social media fans had identified as being served at the same driving range Norris had used a few days before. The fans had found this out by studying the online menu of the driving range and comparing the images. It was a staggering example of the lengths people go to on social media, and the uncomfortable position this often creates.

The final races of the 2021 season saw another disappointing tenth in Saudi Arabia, followed by a seventh place in Abu Dhabi. Those two results meant Norris finished the season in sixth place in the championship, having been in the top three for the majority of it. Ricciardo was fifth and twelfth in those two races, but for all the hype surrounding his arrival in the team, he finished eighth in the championship, some 45 points behind Norris. Ironically, Sainz's third place in Abu Dhabi – which was overshadowed by Verstappen's controversial victory over Hamilton to lift his first world championship, and the subsequent fall-out involving race director Michael Masi – saw him pip Norris to fifth.

THE MONACO MOVE

Over the winter, Norris completed his move to Monaco, and in the 98 days between the final race of 2021 in Abu Dhabi and the season opener in Bahrain in 2022, he had another reason to celebrate. On 9 February, just two days before McLaren launched their 2022 challenger, he signed a new and improved deal to stay with McLaren, a deal that would stretch to four years. It was unprecedented, normally the press are tipped off that contracts are about to be extended or cancelled, but this came out of the blue, especially seeing as last deal was just nine months old.

According to rumours, the contract was worth over £50 million. His Monaco move just got a whole load smarter. He took part in a Zoom call with journalists, during which he explained that part of the thinking of the deal until 2025 was to show his commitment to the team, even if that did kill off interest from the likes of Red Bull, Mercedes or Ferrari. 'I am extremely happy,' he said. 'McLaren is a big part of my career and my life, so to stay for another four years is pretty amazing. McLaren are people I've grown up with. The people I've come into Formula One with. More than anything, we'd love to continue what we have and try and reach that dream of ours, which is to get back to winning races and to eventually try and win championships. This deal is more about solidarity, for me and the team and that level of confidence in both of us. I see it as a benefit for myself to have this longer contract and for the team, it is a performance benefit and motivation. I want to give the whole team the confidence that I'm here to stay. I want to keep trying to achieve things with them.'

It did not feel like PR speak, even if it sounded like it. There was a real feeling that Norris had bought into the McLaren philosophy. He felt comfortable within the team's structure, so much so that he had been willing to turn his back on potential moves to Red Bull or Mercedes – teams with a recent history of delivering cars capable of winning championships. He revealed that there were discussions with other teams but that he had reported the details of the discussions straight back to Brown or Seidl. 'There were other opportunities [elsewhere] that I knew would be coming up in the future with various teams,' said Norris, 'but this put out a strong message on how I believe in McLaren, even with those opportunities that could arise. I had to weigh up all the factors and I looked at all the best options for me in what I think I can achieve. Of course there will now be opportunities for other drivers to go to Red Bull or Mercedes, who knows if I would have had those opportunities. But the fact I chose to stay at McLaren is the good thing about this and is the strong message.'

Seidl confirmed that Norris' new deal did not contain any 'get outs for both sides', which is unusual for an F1 deal that normally contains a host of exit and performance-related clauses. 'The beauty of this new agreement that we have in place is that there are no get outs on both sides,' he said, 'which is simply the important message that we wanted to give to the team.'

There is no doubt that seeing Norris, as well as several other key employees, including Brown, tie their futures to the team, had a positive impact at the team's factory. There was a feverish sense of excitement when they launched their 2022 F1 car at the MTC on Friday 11 February. To their credit, McLaren was one of the only teams to do a physical car launch, alongside Alpine. Instead of hosting an event to see the car and speak to the drivers, every other team simply released computer-generated images of what their cars would look like. Hardly the same, especially when it comes to getting access to the drivers. From a media perspective, it is great to be able to ask drivers a range of questions, and for them to deliver actual answers rather than using dull quotes extracted from press releases.

Speaking to Norris at the MTC, what we got was a driver who had found his voice and was comfortable speaking about other topics, which was the case when he eloquently spoke about F1's decision to alter their pre-race anti-racism message. By saying that he couldn't 'accept doing nothing' to promote diversity, it was clear to see just how far Norris had come with feeling comfortable speaking about serious issues aside from racing. He was blossoming not only as a driver but also as a person. This was the start of a new era of F1, with a radical redesign of the cars as the sport underwent its biggest shake-up in decades. And in the space of just a few months, Norris had signed a lucrative new long-term contract with McLaren, had got a new girlfriend and a new home in Monaco.

Over the winter, confidence at McLaren was high. New sponsors had been secured and their driver pairing was looking solid. There was none of the nervousness that is sometimes displayed by teams when the season kicks off with testing in Barcelona. The winter test offered the first glimpse of how teams had interpreted the new rules for 2022, and it provided the opportunity to assess what team had done the best in terms of new designs.

But while testing is a good chance to see some early running, you never know for sure just how quick a team are going to be until they reach the first qualifying session of the season – in this case the Bahrain Grand Prix. And that is exactly what Norris found as he started his 2022 campaign. In Barcelona on day one, he topped the time sheets, using the C4 soft tyres to leapfrog Leclerc with a lap time of 1 minute, 19.568 seconds, which was 0.597 seconds faster than the Ferrari man. Not only was Norris' time the quickest, but he also enjoyed largely trouble-free running in Spain. But for a brief stop at the pit lane exit, he was untroubled by mechanical issues.

However, it was a different story a few weeks later in Bahrain for the final three days of testing before the start of the new season. With teammate Ricciardo sidelined with Covid-19, Norris was given the responsibility of driving the team's car for all three days. But the early optimism from Barcelona quickly dried up in the desert. On day one, McLaren struggled, with Norris finishing the day in sixth place. The following day, Norris stopped in the pit lane and by the time the session was over, he was only in P7. By the final day, he was even further adrift down in ninth place and was left explaining how the three days had been 'less than ideal' preparation for the new season. He delivered an honest assessment in the paddock, saying, 'it's not been the smoothest of tests for us'. He added: 'Barcelona was a good one, but here we've encountered quite a few more problems, which have limited the number of laps we've done by quite a huge amount. We're behind where we want to be, where we need to be, and where we can say we're confident in any way going into the first race. It's not great but we're getting through as much as we can. We're definitely making progress, but definitely not in the position we want to be in.'

Things got worse after the season-opener where Norris struggled to qualify in thirteenth place and ultimately finished down in fifteenth. He was unable to hold back his disappointment in the post-race media pen as he flippantly responded to a question about his performance. 'Amazing race really. Really enjoyed it,' he said sarcastically.

The following week in Saudi Arabia, he was relaxed when I spoke to him, mainly because the conversation was predominately about golf. He'd played a lot in the Middle East and had shot his personal best in Dubai some four days earlier with a round of 86. His handicap had dropped to fifteen but was due to be cut again once he'd managed to submit a few more scorecards. The chat about golf offered a welcome distraction and rekindled some of the excitement he'd shown at the start of the year heading into the season.

Norris had learned to play golf in West Byfleet, despite the prestigious New Zealand Golf Club being on his doorstep when he was living in Addlestone, while Wentworth was also close by. He still plays the odd game at West Byfleet when he's been to McLaren's MTC before heading back to Monaco. He was asked by another journalist what it was that had attracted him to the game. 'I like competitiveness and striving for perfection,' he said. 'It is the same as racing. Striving to want to do better and improve. It's amazing how something so simple can bring such satisfaction. I'm still so much in a range of making improvements – I probably had one of the worst games in my life the other day playing with Carlos – I was like, "Why do I play golf?" Carlos is very good. He has been playing for ten years. It is just a lot of time, but I'm making improvements. I spend a lot of time looking at videos of my swing, plus I have been playing with the professionals. I played with Ian Poulter. I also played with Bernd Wiesberger, and he is a big F1 fan as well, and his caddy was a really nice guy. I actually played the pro-am with them, which was really cool but then I spent some time on the range and a few of the pros were coming over. I basically spent a whole day on the range. Every now and then, one of the pros will come over and go and say, "Hi, nice to meet you, let's see your swing." And they tried to give me a few pointers. So that day, I probably played the best I've ever done. I was happiest. I'd spent a while in Dubai. All these pros coming over. And then the next day, I tried to play again, and it was one of the worst days of my life! I was like, "I'm so stuck, why can't I do this?! I frickin' hate it." So I decided I'm not going to listen to anyone apart from my coach.'

When the conversation returned to McLaren's struggles in Bahrain, Norris was pragmatic. This was supposed to be the season in which he would kick on and, if he had a degree of good fortune, he would again find himself in a position to be fighting for a victory. However, even at that early stage of the season, his answers and body language showed there was a long season ahead. Having said that, with the ink still drying on his lucrative contract with McLaren, there was no sense that he had any regrets about having committed to such a lengthy deal. Taking it all in his stride, the disappointment about starting the new season on the back foot was understandable, but he did not feel any negativity towards his team. 'I'm here at McLaren for another five years,' he said, 'so there's just no benefit from kicking off. I'm frustrated. Of course, like you saw [in Bahrain] I was frustrated and I want to be trying to score points. I want to be winning races. If I can't win, I want a podium. If I can't be on a podium, I need a top five. If you can't be in the top five. You want to be in the top ten. I guess there's more to a driver than just wanting success and the other half of that is understanding how to be part of the team and optimise everything when you can't win races and you can't have podiums and top tens. But this is still a place I'm learning, and I am discovering more about how we need to work. Hopefully, more of it will pay off when the time comes for us to start scoring highly again.'

Norris also dismissed the theory that the team's poor start was down to the fact that neither driver no longer lived close to the factory. 'I've already been to the factory more this year than I have previously in the past two years,' he said. 'I am still spending a lot of days on the simulator. Whenever McLaren needs me, then I know, I have got to go. That's part of it. Moving to Monaco has made no difference. We kind of knew where we might be, but I guess it was a reality for everyone else watching back at home, where we actually were in relation to the rest of the field, so tough to take but also the realisation of where we were.'

The following day, the racing took a back seat as thick clouds of smoke were seen in the distance behind the Jeddah Corniche Circuit midway through practice. As we looked on social media, it quickly became apparent that there had been a drone strike on a local oil depot. Just a few days earlier, when I was in Bahrain and writing my race report, I had filed a small article about how the Saudi Grand Prix would be targeted by rebels opposed to the regime. I had been monitoring how strategic sites in Saudi were being targeted by pilots of unmanned drones that could be flown into areas to cause disruption or destruction. That is what happened in Jeddah when a facility was targeted by Yemen's Houthi rebels, who claimed responsibility for the attack.

But what happened next was unprecedented. F1 is no stranger when it comes to grappling with security and safety issues. I was in Bahrain in 2012 when certain teams were caught up in attacks between police and protestors in which petrol bombs had been used that had left staff members shaken up. Similarly, in recent years, doubt has been cast over the safety of holding the grand prix in Brazil after team members had been the victims of armed robberies. There have also been conversations about extreme weather and its impact on track safety at numerous races. But before Saudi, there had never been a wide-scale security threat leading all drivers to demand assurances of their safety.

That Friday evening in Jeddah, all twenty drivers, and F1's CEO Stefano Domenicali and managing director Ross Brawn, got together behind closed doors to discuss their concerns about racing. The meeting lasted for over four hours. Obviously, Norris was part of the discussions along with the other members of the Grand Prix Drivers' Association. It was left to George Russell as a director of the association to announce that the drivers would not be boycotting the race, having been assured of their safety. However, there were suggestions that the drivers were warned that there would be consequences should they not fulfil their obligation to race for their teams in this round of the F1 championship. It seemed a rather heavy-handed approach to persuade the drivers to go ahead and compete. The whole episode left a bad taste in the mouth, and the future of the Saudi date was called into question pending further talks between F1, the FIA and the drivers. As for the race itself, Norris qualified in eleventh and finished seventh, while Ricciardo suffered a DNF as his McLaren had a problem with overheating.

At the fourth race of the season, there was renewed enthusiasm within the McLaren camp as Norris took another podium – the sixth of his career. In the previous race in Australia, he finished a credible fifth, while Ricciardo was sixth, despite the performance of the McLaren cars being some way behind Red Bull and Ferrari.

At this point in the season, 'porpoising' had become an issue for all teams, a term used to describe how the cars would bounce up and down as a result of unstable aerodynamics. When air is sucked underneath a car, it pulls it down closer to the track; and the faster the car goes, the nearer it gets to the track. However, there reaches a point where the airflow stops, causing a stall, and the downforce stops and the car springs back up again. The increase in distance between the car's floor and the track means the process begins again, which leads to constant bouncing at high speed. Porpoising was not only uncomfortable, it was also becoming dangerous as some drivers were bouncing about so much in the cockpit that it became difficult for them to see.

But by the time the fourth race at Imola came around, McLaren were on top of the problem and were able to take an unlikely podium finish. After crossing the line, Norris praised McLaren's teamwork after a difficult start to 2022. The Brit had benefited after Leclerc hit the barriers in his pursuit for third place, which ended up promoting Norris. 'Amazing race, amazing weekend to be honest,' said Norris after the race. 'To beat one Red Bull and a Ferrari is much more than we were expecting. I'm happy. The team deserves it. From where we were in race one to now scoring a podium, they all deserve it, so top job to the team. This weekend, it wasn't necessarily all about the car. A lot of it was [down to] the teamwork, the pit stop was amazing and just how we executed the weekend, which is what gave us this result. With the start, the strategy, the qualifying, judging the tyres and all of this stuff – the smaller things that you don't get to see – it's what got us this podium, so it's lovely to see.'

The relief was obvious after tough races in Bahrain, Saudi and Australia, but Norris was also keeping his expectations in check. 'We worked so hard in Bahrain, and we got so little out of it,' he added. 'And even the more effort we put into the last few races, it's nice to see it paying off in a way. Honestly, we brought some small things, but nothing that has boosted us into P3. I don't believe we had the third-best car behind Red Bull and Ferrari. The Alfa Romeo was extremely fast as well. The improvements we've been bringing are definitely moving us forward, slowly forward, and we definitely need to try and keep that up.'

Zak Brown was also aware of the fact his team was not really in a position to contend with Red Bull or Ferrari and was not getting ahead of himself. In an interview with the *Daily Telegraph* after the race in Imola and ahead of the inaugural Miami GP, he spoke of the two teams ahead of him: 'I think they have got this season locked down. I think by mid-season you could see the field a lot tighter and maybe some others winning. Ferrari and Red Bull are going to have such a head start for the first ten races that even if others start catching up by mid-year, like what happened with Brawn [in 2009], it will be too late from a championship perspective.'

When asked about Norris and how he compared to Leclerc and Verstappen, Brown was emphatic: 'As a driver and a talent? No question. We see Lando in that bracket. He's mega. Totally mega.' The conversation then switched to whether McLaren could deliver a car that Norris could use to showcase his talent. 'I don't want to make excuses,' he began, 'but right now, we're behind and we know why; we don't have the technical infrastructure that the others have. But for the 2024 season? In theory there will be no excuses left other than it's damn tough and there are four or five other teams that have no excuses. He committed to us long term precisely because he can see himself winning a world championship with us. As long as we continue to move forward, I think he's happy. He loves the environment here; the family. Lando has been with us from day one. So I think while he'd love to win the world championship today, as long as we're moving forward, I think he's happy to come on the journey. He's still only 22, remember.'

But if McLaren or Norris were having ambitious thoughts about radical improvements, they were brought back down to earth at the Miami Grand Prix. Norris suffered a retirement in an otherwise dreary race. Afterwards, he clarified what had happened, saying, 'everyone thought I hit a wall, but I just spun.

It was just a surprise how quickly it happened. With the people around me I expected someone hitting me, but it just felt like a fast spin really. Nothing bad,' he added. And once again, Norris sought to temper hopes that the team had started to unlock the potential of their race car: 'We have to be careful. It wasn't like we were bringing massive upgrades every weekend and making loads of progress. We brought a couple of [new] things [for the car], but it didn't make us go from being 1.5 seconds off in Bahrain to half a second. The tracks are a much bigger deciding factor than anything else. We understand that we might be better and have a chance of going to Q3 and so on, but we won't be going back there and fighting for podiums, like we did at Imola.'

By the time the Monaco GP came around, it had become clear that Ricciardo was again struggling to keep up with Norris. The highs from his win in Monza in 2021 had since dissipated – even though Brown would carry the tattoo on his arm for the rest of his life. Norris was still delivering, while the Australian's only points finish had come in his home race; and that was only sixth place behind Norris in fifth. Ricciardo's body language spoke volumes, and he had clearly lost some confidence. He was obviously struggling for form and was seemingly unable to turn around the run of poor results.

Meanwhile, Norris knew he had the better of his teammate as he relished his first of two home races in the calendar, in his new Riviera home town, even though he was suffering from a bout of tonsilitis Norris finished sixth. 'I am enjoying it there [in Monaco],' he said in his column in the *Daily Telegraph* a few days after the race, in which he spoke about adjusting to life in Monaco. 'I am not sure that I am yet comfortable calling it a home race. Silverstone is my home race. But the experience of living there and racing there was nice. It is such a different feeling going back to your own bed. A two-minute scooter ride into the track each morning. It really helped after the week

I had. I was diagnosed with tonsillitis on the Thursday of the previous race in Barcelona [where he had finished in eighth place] and my symptoms got progressively worse through that race weekend: cold sweats, fever, aching muscles. By Sunday, my throat was so sore it was like swallowing daggers. I could barely drink because it hurt so much. I was lucky that my trainer and team doctor came and stayed with me in Monaco. By Thursday, when my parents arrived, I was just about back up and running, although I did cancel all of my media commitments as I could barely speak. In the end, it turned into a magical weekend, and having my parents and my girlfriend staying with me made it all the more special. Not that I celebrated. I do not really drink at the best of times. If I ever win a race, they are going to have to find me something other than champagne, as I cannot stand the stuff. Instead, I went back to my flat and had a quiet night in watching the Indy 500.'

I caught up with Norris ahead of the British Grand Prix. I had travelled to the MTC to see him and he had just flown in from Monaco. He'd previously finished ninth in Azerbaijan and fifteenth in Canada, so recent form was not a topic we focused on. Instead, I wanted to ask him about the increase in attention he had received ahead of his proper home race. His social media following had continued to grow, and he had carved out a reputation as everyone's second-favourite driver. However, despite the positive outward demeanour, it turned out that both Norris and his girlfriend Luisinha had been receiving a staggering amount of online abuse. He explained that while he was getting used to it, it was difficult for the Portuguese model, who had been thrust into the limelight when their relationship became public.

'The amount of hate pages dedicated to Luisinha now, it is pretty horrific,' he explained. 'They are on Instagram and Twitter, It is not an easy thing because if you come from a different life to Formula One, it is a big contrast. Having a normal life to all of a sudden having lots of followers, she has to be more careful about what she says and does. In racing, you go through it a bit more slowly and you learn to adapt to it – between Formula Four to Formula Three and up to Formula Two. Formula One's a big step, but for her, she'd never watched a race before and suddenly being in that limelight is extremely tough for someone to go through and the amount of comments she gets – and I want to protect her.'

In the run up to his home race, Norris was excited to see the crowds. Despite being less competitive in the previous two races, he knew that the support would give him a boost. There were upgrades for the car, and the surface and track characteristics would be different at Silverstone to those in Canada. Lando had also played rounds of golf with Ian Poulter and Justin Rose in the run up to the British race and revealed he was using the sport as a way of mentally resetting and coping with the pressure of racing in F1. 'Taking up golf has helped me a lot,' he said. 'When you can go out there and it's just you, the club and the ball, you stop thinking about all the other problems. It's so difficult, all you're thinking about is your swing or where to place the ball to strive to be more perfect than last time. From a mental side it is absolutely helping me. It's extremely different to F1, but the one thing it has in common is the constant strive for perfection. Golf teaches you to deal with frustration quickly, to put it behind you and driving is the same.'

But for the online abuse, which even extended to death threats, Norris was conscious that he was nonetheless one of the most popular drivers on the grid. 'I just need to win some races,' he said. 'I'm just normal, in a way, but it's hard to continue to be like that in the world of Formula One. I would probably stream more on Twitch, and I'd still do a lot more of these things … In some sports you are able to train 24/7. I can't just go and pick up a Formula One car and go and drive all the time. There's only so much you can do and there's only so much training physically you want to do, but you also need time to rest and enjoy your life.'

He had managed the move to Monaco and his relationship seemed to be going well. He was also beating his teammate, the only yardstick that really mattered. 'I'm in the most comfortable position I've been in a while,' he added. 'But having that experience of so many fans – like on the fan stage with everyone chanting – it is a special feeling because you'd never expect that, growing up, I never did. Those people are all there supporting me and waiting for me to do a good job, so that is such a cool thing' … I do seem to have a lot of fans everywhere I go. Whether it is in Italy or Spain, obviously the Belgium side of things is always good for me. Everywhere I go, I get a decent amount of supporters. I think being in a team that is not fighting for a championship straightaway has helped that … I just hope everyone continues to support me and I continue to grow my fan base because I want that. The more the merrier.'

The question marks surrounding Ricciardo's future in the team were intensifying. It seemed unthinkable that his future was being debated after he had earned the team their first win in years. He had received a rather public dressing-down from Brown, who had said in no uncertain terms that he needed to start delivering on a regular basis. Ricciardo's contract ran until the end of 2023, but there had been mounting speculation that he would be replaced by American driver Colton Herta, who had a two-day test for McLaren in Portimão. IndyCar champion Alex Palou had also joined the team's ranks, so it was not surprising that rumours were spreading that Ricciardo was on his way out. After all, by the halfway point of the season, Norris had out-qualified Ricciardo at nine of the eleven races and scored 47 points more. Yet the Australian was defiant and took to Instagram to address the speculation: 'There have been a lot of rumours around my future in Formula One, but I want you to hear it from me. I am committed to McLaren until the end of next year and am not walking away from the sport. Appreciate it hasn't always been easy, but who wants easy? I'm working my arse off with the team to make improvements and get the car right and back to the front where it belongs. I still want this more than ever. See you [at the next race] in Le Castellet.'

Unfortunately, nothing much changed in France and Ricciardo was again beaten by Norris, who was seventh to the Australian's ninth place. The same applied in Hungary where Norris was again seventh, while Ricciardo was fifteenth. Before the Belgian Grand Prix, McLaren had obviously seen enough, and it was announced that Ricciardo's deal would be terminated after the two parties agreed a settlement. Ricciardo described the decision as 'bittersweet' and suggested that he had been willing to stick it out, although McLaren insisted their parting had been mutual. 'I have some news to share and it's not great, bittersweet for sure, but I think it's best to hear from me. 2022 will be my last year with McLaren,' Ricciardo said. 'We put in a lot of effort on both sides, but it hasn't worked the way we wanted, so the team decided to make a change for next year and we had a lot of discussions. But in the end, we mutually agreed that it was the right thing.'

The announcement came a month on from the Australian's social media posts claiming that he was committed to seeing out his contract. It was expected that he would be replaced by fellow countryman Oscar Piastri, although he too had a contract in place with Alpine. Everything had become rather confusing as Alpine had recently announced that Piastri would be replacing Alonso, who was joining Aston Martin. Yet Piastri put out his own message on social media stating that he would not be joining Alpine. What followed was a complicated tug of war that would come to play out during the Dutch Grand Prix, but it was Ricciardo's future that became the main focus in the media. 'If you look back at the last eighteen months of our journey together, it's clear we haven't achieved the result we wanted, despite highlights like the great win in Monza last year,' Seidl said. 'That's why we had a lot of discussions, but in the end, we had to acknowledge we did not make it work together despite the commitment that was there from Daniel's side and all the effort the team has put in. We tried everything from both sides; unfortunately, we couldn't make it work, which is also my responsibility.'

Norris was asked about Ricciardo's situation for the first time at the Belgian Grand Prix, and he gave an honest assessment. Asked if he had any sympathy for Ricciardo, Norris said: 'I hate to say it, but I would say no. People will probably hate me for saying it and it's difficult because I never know if I might encounter that in the future with this car or a different team, so I never want to contradict myself going into the future. I've just got to focus on my driving and my job. It's not my job to focus on someone else and I'm not a driver coach. I'm not here to help and do those kinds of things.'

Norris was also quizzed on Piastri, as he awaited confirmation that he would be allowed to join McLaren by Formula One's Contract Recognition Board. I asked Norris if he had been consulted over Piastri's signing, and his response was interesting. 'In a way, yes,' he said. 'Some of the drivers on their list, they've said, "What do you think of him?" But I don't have a final say. I don't know Oscar that well, but he is good friends with some of my friends because he was there in the Renault Academy. From what I've heard, he is a lovely guy and works hard. And from what I've seen, he's very talented, extremely quick. Whoever it is, I'll welcome them to the team and look forward to working with them. I don't mind as long as I can get along with them.' Piastri was eventually granted permission to join McLaren for 2023 – much to the frustration of Alpine. The move was confirmed on 2 September 2022 after Alpine lost their appeal to F1's Contract Recognition Board (CRB). Alpine had lodged a claim with the board but the lawyers adjudicating the dispute for the CRB rejected their argument that Piastri was committed to them. He was subsequently free to join McLaren.

Ricciardo's departure was not the only break-up that summer, as Norris split from girlfriend Luisinha. While their relationship had been kept quiet initially, the public announcement that they were together had only been made at the start of 2022. There was no hint of any animosity, for they had spent summer on holiday together, but Norris confirmed that they had decided to go their separate ways on Instagram. 'Hello everyone,' he wrote. 'After time and consideration, Luisa and myself have mutually decided to end our relationship but remain good friends. I wish her the world and have so much respect for her and all she does as an amazing and strong woman with nothing but kindness. Please respect our decision and respect our but more importantly and especially her privacy moving forward. Thank you for your endless support.'

Norris had a solid end to the 2022 season, the highlight being a fourth-place finish in Singapore, while at the Japanese Grand Prix he had a run-in with Max Verstappen during qualifying, which got quite heated. Norris was angry after a near-miss with the Dutchman, who later accused the McLaren driver of a lack of 'respect'.

But the two had buried the hatchet by the time they flew back to Monaco after the race, with Norris performing a DJ set at Verstappen's title-celebration party. Norris had taken up his new hobby and had been posting images across his social media of him at the decks. He spent a few days in Brazil honing his musical skills ahead of the grand prix, but picked up a bout of food poisoning, which threatened to ruin his weekend. Somehow, he managed to combat the sickness to qualify in fourth place for the sprint race. In the main event, his misery was compounded by a gearbox failure on lap 53 that put him out. To add insult to injury, George Russell claimed his maiden victory, and while Norris was pleased for his fellow Brit, there was a sense of frustration that he was unable to get that win that had eluded him in Russia. Catching up with Norris at the final race of the year in Abu Dhabi, he said: 'Anytime someone wins the race, I'm jealous of it. I'm happy for him. Of course, there's some jealousy but it gives me more confidence at the same time. I feel if I was in that position [to fight for a win], that I could do something very similar, so I look forward to hopefully being in that fight.'

During the same interview in the Abu Dhabi paddock, Norris reflected on the year that had passed. While it had not yielded his first victory, he was in a reflective mood and had reasons to feel optimistic about his future in the team, for they had made good progress from the opening race of the season, despite ultimately playing catch-up to their rivals for the rest of the season. 'There's different parts to it all,' he said. 'If I start with the bad ones. I don't think we were ever that good in Barcelona. We just had a car that we put on track and we optimised it within a few runs. We got that too quickly so we hit our limit very early on. We went to Bahrain and we started off poorly, it was just pretty horrendous. We then had a turnaround and I think the team did a good job to fix the issues around the brakes and reliability proved to be one of our biggest strengths. I think we developed reasonably well for the next half of the season, the main thing is we started the year off with a car which was just too far under the limit. There are a lot of things that we've done well. Our pit stops have been some of the quickest and from the strategy side of things, we've done a very good job optimising the car. Then from my side, by far this has been my best season in Formula One in terms of being able to deliver every weekend in qualifying and by not making so many big mistakes in the race. Hopefully, next year we will be in the best place we have ever been, but we will have to take a big step if we want to be close to challenging the top teams.'

Over the winter and coming into 2023, there were again reports that Norris was being eyed by Red Bull as a replacement for Sergio Pérez, while Hamilton's future at Mercedes led to rumours that the Silver Arrows were considering a move for the McLaren driver. The vacuum of any real news in the off-season turned the internet into an echo chamber of speculation, but while he was still without a win, Norris had shown enough in his four seasons in F1 that he was fully deserving of his place at motor sport's top table. He had gone toe-to-toe with Sainz and comfortably seen off the challenge from Ricciardo.

In an interview with *GQ*, he addressed Ricciardo's departure. 'Carlos and I get on extremely well,' he explained. 'I kind of grew up with him. Daniel I got on with pretty well. He and I were the perfect competitors: we hated beating each other like we hated getting beat by one another. Away from the track we respected each other massively. I keep it separate; I can be the biggest competitor I need to be on the racetrack, but I can also respect and be good mates with other people.'

However, for the 2023 season, he would be going up against an unknown in Oscar Piastri. But the reservations expressed by the team at the launch of their new car for the season were more of a concern for Norris than his new driver pairing. The pre-recorded show at the MTC was slick, but in the interview session afterwards, the team's new principal Andrea Stella said he was 'happy but not entirely happy with the launch car'; however, he was still 'optimistic' that steps could be made as McLaren were still waiting for their new wind tunnel and simulator to be completed, which would be used in the development of their 2024 car. 'Normally, you need to be totally happy to achieve your targets,' said Stella. 'While we are happy with the development in most areas, there are some areas where we realised some strong directions a little late so have not necessarily been able to capitalise in the short term. That's why I talk about "after the start of the season". It is more relative to ourselves and that's why I talk about realism.' He added: 'I think it's fair to say that over the course of the season we would like to establish ourselves as part of the top four. We know realistically that with the top three teams, this may mean potentially just being the fourth best car, like I say, over the course of the season, we are realistic in the very short term.'

Norris said he too had the patience to wait for McLaren's rebuilding process to be completed. 'We are a team who should be able to win championships and we will soon have everything in place to do so,' he explained. He also reinforced the message that he had 'definitely not lost faith', adding: 'I am probably not the most patient guy in the world, but it is something you need to learn to have in F1. I am just doing my job one day at a time and that's the way I go about it. A successful year would be to still take some big steps forward, a year where we can get back to fighting at the front of the midfield confidently – that's something that slipped away from us last year – and leading the fight for the top three teams. If we can end this season around that spot, where we are fighting for fourth constructor and leading the way to the top three, we can be happy. That is a realistic goal. You can't expect us to be level with Red Bull and Ferrari and Mercedes this year, there is still a way to go for that.'

His contract with McLaren runs until the end of the 2025 season and both he and the team know that the clock is ticking to start delivering. Unless Norris is given a competitive car capable of fighting for championships, McLaren could risk losing their rising star to a competitor. For as his racing career has shown, Lando Norris has the potential to be the very best in the world.

LANDO NORRIS PROFESSIONAL RACING RECORD

2013

CIK WORLD KF JUNIOR, RICKY FLYNN MOTORSPORT Win, pole position, fastest lap

CIK-FIA KF JUNIOR SUPER CUP, RICKY FLYNN MOTORSPORT Win

CIK-FIA EURO KFJ, RICKY FLYNN MOTORSPORT 25 points (1 win), champion

2014

GINETTA JUNIOR, HHC MOTORSPORT 4 wins, 11 podiums, 8 pole positions, 2 fastest laps, 432 points, 3rd overall

CIK-FIA WORLD KF, RICKY FLYNN MOTORSPORT Win, fastest lap

CIK-FIA EURO KF, RICKY FLYNN MOTORSPORT 1 podium, 2 fastest laps, 64 points, 3rd overall

2015

MSA FORMULA, CARLIN 8 wins, 15 podiums, 5 pole positions, 9 fastest laps, 413 points, champion

BRDC F4 AT, HHC MOTORSPORT 4 races, 2 wins, 4 podiums, 1 pole position, 1 fastest lap, 128 points, 5th overall

F4 ITALY, MÜCKE MOTORSPORT 9 races, 1 podium, 3 fastest laps, 51 points, 11th overall

ADAC F4, ADAC BERLIN-BRANDENBURG E.V. 8 races, 1 win, 6 podiums, 2 fastest laps, 131 points, 8th overall

2016

F3 MACAU, CARLIN 11th

F.RENAULT 2.0 EURO, JOSEF KAUFMANN RACING 5 wins, 12 podiums, 6 pole positions, 4 fastest laps, 253 points, champion

F.RENAULT 2.0 NEC, JOSEF KAUFMANN RACING 6 wins, 11 podiums, 10 pole positions, 4 fastest laps, 326 points, champion

TOYOTA RACING SERIES NZ, M2 COMPETITION 6 wins, 11 podiums, 8 pole positions, 5 fastest laps, 924 points, champion

BRDC F3, CARLIN 11 races, 4 wins, 8 podiums, 4 pole positions, 3 fastest laps, 247 points, 8th overall

FIA F3 EURO, CARLIN 3 races

MEMBER BRDC Rising Stars

2017

FIA FORMULA 2, CAMPOS RACING 2 races, 0 points, 25th overall

FIA F3 EURO, CARLIN 9 wins, 20 podiums, 8 pole positions, 8 fastest laps, 441 points, champion,

F3 MACAU, CARLIN 2nd

FIA F3 EURO TESTS, CARLIN 6 days, 2,317 kilometres

FIA F2 TESTS, CAMPOS RACING

F1 TESTS, MCLAREN HONDA 2 days, 1,054 kilometres

MEMBER BRDC SuperStars

MEMBER McLaren Young Driver Programme

2018

FORMULA 1, MCLAREN F1 TEAM

FIA FORMULA 2, CARLIN 1 win, 9 podiums, 1 pole position, 1 fastest lap, 219 points, 2nd overall

DAYTONA 24H (P), UNITED AUTOSPORTS 38th

IMSA SC (P), UNITED AUTOSPORTS 1 race, 18 points, 58th overall

F1 TESTS, MCLAREN F1 TEAM 5 days, 2,270 kilometres

FIA F2 TESTS, CARLIN

2019

FORMULA 1, MCLAREN F1 TEAM 49 points, 11th overall

F1 TESTS, MCLAREN F1 TEAM 8 days, 3,270 kilometres

2020

FORMULA 1, MCLAREN F1 TEAM 1 podium, 2 fastest laps, 97 points, 9th overall

F1 TESTS, MCLAREN F1 TEAM 4 days, 1,657 kilometres

[ESPORTS] F1 VIRTUAL, MCLAREN F1 TEAM 2 fastest laps, 31 points, 8th overall

[ESPORTS] LM 24H VIRTUAL (LMP), TEAM REDLINE 25th overall

[ESPORTS] INDYCAR IRACING, INDYCAR PROVISIONAL, ARROW MCLAREN SP 2 race, 1 win, 1 pole position, 1 fastest lap

[ESPORTS] SUPERCARS ES, MOBIL 1 ARROW RACING 9 races, 1 win, 2 podiums, 393 points, 27th overall

2021

FORMULA 1, MCLAREN F1 TEAM 4 podiums, 1 pole position, 1 fastest lap, 160 points, 6th overall

F1 TESTS, MCLAREN F1 TEAM 4 days, 1,377 kilometres

2022

FORMULA 1, MCLAREN F1 TEAM 1 podium, 2 fastest laps, 122 points, 7th overall

F1 TESTS, MCLAREN F1 TEAM 6 days, 2,414 kilometres

Awards and honours

Autosport British Club Driver of the Year: 2016
McLaren Autosport BRDC Award: 2016
Autosport National Driver of the Year: 2017
Autosport British Competition Driver of the Year: 2019
Autosport British Competition Driver of the Year: 2020
Autosport British Competition Driver of the Year: 2021

Career F1 statistics
(as of the end of the 2022 season)

85 grands prix (85 starts)
0 wins
6 podiums
436 career points
1 pole positions
5 fastest laps

Stats from Forix

ACKNOWLEDGEMENTS

I would like to dedicate this book to my wife, Hayley. Without her love, support, kindness and patience I would not be where I am today. I would also like to take this opportunity to thank her, and my children, Teddy and Rose, for putting up with me and my career.

Covering Formula One is a perpetual balancing act between work and family life, yet they have never once complained about me missing birthdays and special occasions.

Thanks to Mum and Dad for supplying tea and biscuits for when I was writing this book during my off-season. To them, and to Dave and Maggie, for stepping in and helping out when I am away with work.

A big-up to Sim and Lucy for helping me stay on top of my crazy mind. For Melanie, my agent, for asking me to undertake this title.

I'd also like to thank those who have contributed to this book especially Charlotte and those at ADD Management.

To Lando for answering all my questions every Thursday during race weekends and to all the McLaren Comms team for allowing it.

Finally, to the esteemed members of 'The Groovy Gang'. Thanks for making the time away from home more bearable .

The bestselling biography of Formula 1's double world champion.

Few drivers have ever shaken up Formula 1 in quite the same way as Max Verstappen. Already the youngest competitor in F1 history, having made his breakthrough in 2015 aged just seventeen, he has gone on to make history as the first Dutch driver to win the World Championship. In 2022 he retained his title with four races to spare and went on to achieve the highest season points tally of all time.

Sports journalist James Gray seeks to understand the outspoken nature and aggressive driving style that make Verstappen a must-watch before, during and after races, and why his Dutch fans, who turn up to cheer him on in their orange-clad droves, are quite so fanatical.

ISBN 978-178578-919-9 (paperback)
ISBN 978-178578-731-7 (eBook)

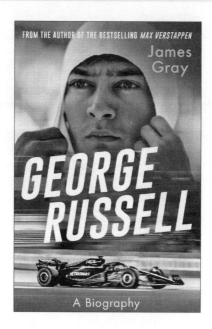

The very first biography of George Russell by the author of the bestselling _Max Verstappen_.

From dominating the karting tracks of East Anglia to the top of Formula 3 and Formula 2, George Russell has established himself as a rising Formula 1 star.

After cutting his teeth with Williams, in 2022 he signed a lucrative contract with Mercedes, where he has been confirmed as the successor to Lewis Hamilton. But will he manage to follow in the footsteps of the greatest F1 driver ever?

Sports journalist James Gray traces how George Russell has been setting the racing track alight since the age of seven and how he is now destined to become the heir apparent to the crown of British racing.

ISBN 978-183773-010-0 (paperback)
ISBN 978-183773-011-7 (eBook)

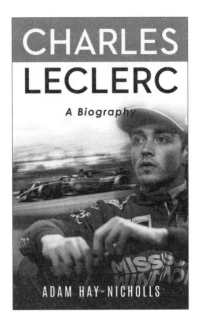

From acclaimed journalist Adam Hay-Nicholls, the very first biography of Charles Leclerc.

Few of the drivers on the F1 grid have the racing pedigree of Charles Leclerc. Now firmly established as Ferrari's great hope, following in the footsteps of legends Ascari, Lauda and Schumacher, Leclerc has his eyes set on becoming world champion.

Born in Monaco to a family of comparatively modest means, Leclerc remembers playing with toy cars on a friend's balcony as F1 drivers whizzed around the Monte Carlo circuit below. This early experience inspired him to get behind the wheel, and so began his meteoric rise in the sport.

Writer Adam Hay-Nicholls provides the inside track on this rising star, recounting how he has taken the racing world by storm.

ISBN 978-183773-008-7 (paperback)
ISBN 978-183773-009-4 (eBook)